W9-ANC-917

The History of
NASA

Ray Spangenburg and Kit Moser

Franklin Watts

A DIVISION OF SCHOLASTIC INC.
NEW YORK · TORONTO · LONDON · AUCKLAND · SYDNEY
MEXICO CITY · NEW DELHI · HONG KONG
DANBURY, CONNECTICUT

For
RAY SPANGENBURG, SR.
Pilot and seeker of dreams

Photographs ©: AP/Wide World Photos: 24; Corbis-Bettmann: 16 (Hulton-Deutsch Collection), 73 (UPI), 39, 48, 106; Finley Holiday Film: 66; Lockheed Martin: 96, 118; NASA: 62, 63, 65, 70, 110 (JPL), cover, 6, 8, 17, 21, 26, 28, 29, 34 left, 37, 46, 49, 51, 53, 57, 68, 72, 77, 79, 83, 87, 89, 94, 98, 99, 105, 109, 114, 121, 122; Photo Researchers: 56 (Mark Marten/NASA), 85, 102 (NASA), 64 (NASA/Science Source), 11 (Novosti/SPL), 80 (SPL); Photri: 22, 34 right, 90.
Map created by Bob Italiano.

Library of Congress Cataloging-in-Publication Data

Spangenburg, Ray.
    The history of NASA / by Ray Spangenburg and Kit Moser.
        p.   cm.—(Out of this world)
    Includes bibliographical references and index.
    Summary: Surveys the history of the National Aeronautics and Space Administration, describing the major spacecraft and missions launched.
    ISBN 0-531-11718-9 (lib. bdg.)   0-531-16511-6 (pbk.)
    1. Astronautics—United States—History Juvenile literature. 2. United States. National Aeronautics and Space Administration—History Juvenile literature. [1. United States. National Aeronautics and Space Administration—History. 3. Outer space—Exploration.] I. Moser, Diane, 1944– . II. Title. III. Series: Out of this world (Franklin Watts, Inc.)
TL789.8.U5S66   2000
629.4'0973—dc21   99-37379

Acknowledgments

A book is the product of many minds and many conversations. The knowledge, expertise, and resources of many people flow into the mix, and we would especially like to thank some of those who have contributed to *The History of NASA.*

First of all, special appreciation goes to Franklin Watts senior science editor Melissa Stewart, whose steady flow of creativity, energy, enthusiasm, and expertise have infused this series. Our thanks also to National Aeronautics and Space Administration (NASA) Chief Historian Roger D. Launius, who reviewed the manuscript and made many useful suggestions.

For stimulating past conversations on the subject of NASA, many thanks to Christopher P. McKay of NASA's Ames Research Center, former astronaut Rusty Schweichart, planetary scientist Mustafa Chahine of the Jet Propulsion Laboratory, and many others who gave generously of their time. Finally, to Tony Reichhardt and John Rhea, our editors at the former *Space World Magazine,* thanks for starting us out on the fascinating journey we have taken during our years of writing about space.

Contents

Apollo 8 astronauts took this picture of Earth rising above the Moon's desolate horizon.

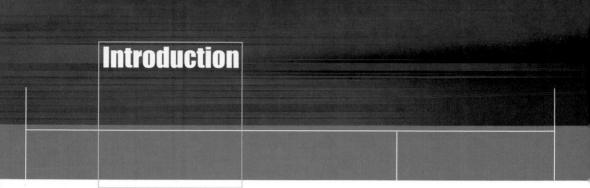

Introduction

"A Grand Oasis"

The space age has dramatically changed the way we view our world. By the mid-1900s, explorers had traveled to every corner of Earth and cartographers had created detailed maps showing its tallest mountains and deepest valleys. We thought we knew our home planet, but we had never seen the big picture. No one was prepared for the staggering beauty of the image we first saw in December 1968.

As the crew of *Apollo 8* headed home after orbiting the Moon, they saw our planet rise above the horizon. No one had ever before witnessed Earthrise. There, cutting an arc against the vast blackness of space, loomed the great curves of a jewel-like globe. Swirling white clouds passed over vast blue waters and greenish-brown landmasses.

The Space Shuttle *Discovery* thunders into space to begin another mission.

It was an amazing view. When the image was released to the world, people stared at it in awe. Suddenly, we came to appreciate the fragility of our tiny planet and its isolation in an infinite Universe. The famous scientist Carl Sagan once called Earth a "pale blue dot." Astronaut Buzz Aldrin called it a "grand oasis."

The *Apollo 8* mission was just one of many, many missions planned and executed by the National Aeronautics and Space Administration (NASA). For more than 40 years, this giant federal agency has led the way to an enormous expansion of knowledge—about Earth, the solar system, and the Universe.

When someone says "NASA," you probably think of cutting-edge technology, robot landers on Mars, and a host of spectacular images sent back from spacecraft roaming the solar system. You may also think of shuttle launches, artificial *satellites*, and people walking on the Moon. The story of NASA isn't just a story about space, though. It's a story of how hardworking scientists and engineers have accomplished amazing feats and how courageous astronauts have braved great dangers. It's a story of dreams and daring visions, of politics and hard realities. It's also the tale of how NASA's work has not only changed our view of the world, but the way we live in it.

First Ventures into Space

For as long as people have looked up at the nighttime sky, they have dreamed of going there. For a long time, though, no one knew how. Countless philosophers and scientists pondered the same question: How could a human being possibly travel beyond Earth's atmosphere? They wondered if anyone would ever figure out a way to visit planets and moons millions of miles away.

By the end of the 1800s, a few talented mathematicians and engineers had some revolutionary insights. They understood how rocket power could propel an object beyond the pull of Earth's gravity. However, not until the mid-1950s did anyone find a way to accomplish this goal.

On October 4, 1957, a team of scientists and engineers in the Soviet Union launched the first human-made satellite into *orbit* around Earth. *Sputnik* winked like a shiny spot of aluminum foil as it arced from horizon to horizon. It beeped radio signals to Earth, like tiny heartbeats from beyond the safe envelope of Earth's atmosphere.

A month later, on November 3, the Soviets had a second success. They sent *Sputnik 2*—and the first living creature—into space. A small dog named Laika was on board.* Putting the 1,121-pound (509-kilogram) satellite into orbit demonstrated that Soviet scientists had tremendous technological expertise. It was clear that the Soviet Union had serious plans for space.

On November 3, 1957, a dog named Laika became the first animal to travel in space. This model shows a model of Laika inside a replica of the Soviet *Sputnik 2* satellite.

Fighting the Cold War in Space

The former Soviet Union, more formally known as the Union of Soviet Socialist Republics (USSR), was formed following the Russian Revolution of 1917. It united Russia, Ukraine, Belarus, and many other countries in Central Asia, Eastern Europe, and the Balkan Peninsula. The Soviet Union's new Communist government quickly became a dictatorship dominated by the Russian Communist Party.

* Laika gave her life in the name of human endeavor. Former Soviet space administrators have since expressed regret about sending Laika into space without getting her back.

Science at Work: What Makes a Rocket Go?

Have you ever blown up a balloon and then let go of it? As you add air to the balloon, the pressure inside builds up. When you let go of the balloon, air rushes out in one direction and the balloon is propelled in the opposite direction.

According to Isaac Newton's third law of motion, for every action there is an equal and opposite reaction. In other words, when something is pushed forward, something else must move backward the same amount. An inflated balloon obeys this law, and so does a gun and an octopus.

When a gun is fired, the force of the exploding gunpowder propels a bullet out of the barrel. At the same time, the gun *recoils* in the opposite direction. The action of the bullet flying out of the gun is balanced by the equal and opposite reaction of the gun's recoil. To move through the ocean, an octopus forcefully expels water in one direction so that its body will be propelled in the opposite direction.

If an octopus could expel water continuously, it would move steadily forward—its movement would be identical to that of a rocket. A rocket releases a steady stream of exhaust. The gas molecules that make up exhaust are produced as fuel burns inside a rocket's engine. The forces of action and reaction, which propel a rocket forward, occur the moment the fuel is burned—before the exhaust leaves the engine.

The movement of a rocket does not depend on anything outside the engine. In other words, a rocket is not propelled forward because its exhaust pushes against air. This is an important idea because space is a *vacuum*—it contains no air. In space, there is absolutely nothing to push against.

According to Newton's first law of motion, an object in motion will stay in motion until it is acted upon by an outside force. On Earth, such forces as gravity and friction affect the movement of objects. These same forces do not act on objects moving through the vacuum of space, however.

An object in space will continue to move in the same direction until it bumps into another object or a push is applied in another direction. This push could come from a *rocket thruster*. If a spacecraft has a rocket thruster on each side and you want it to turn to the right, you would turn on the left thruster.

For many years, the USSR was one of the strongest powers in the world.* During that time, most non-Communist countries viewed its power as an enormous threat to freedom and democracy.

* The Soviet Union dissolved in 1991.

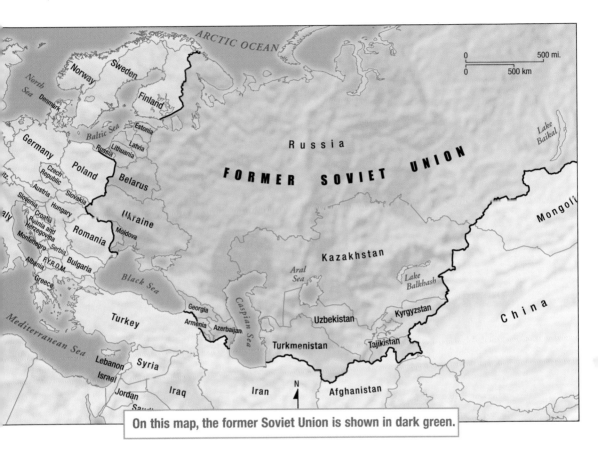

On this map, the former Soviet Union is shown in dark green.

In the years following World War II, the United States and the USSR became increasingly hostile, even though they were not technically at war. Instead, they entered a period known as the Cold War. Although the two world powers rarely fired bullets or bombs at each other, they were very unfriendly and antagonistic. Because each country believed that a "hot," fighting war might break out at any time, they stockpiled nuclear weapons and competed ferociously for worldwide influence and esteem. Both governments strove to prove their superiority. Some of their most bitter rivalry took the form of an immense "space race."

Both the United States and the USSR believed that having superior technology would boost respect for their power and prestige on Earth. After all, rockets that could soar into space could also be aimed, with a warhead attached, at any country in the world.

Trying to Catch Up

With the launch of *Sputnik*, the Soviet Union showed the world that it was clearly ahead of the United States in the space race. The success of *Sputnik* was an enormous embarrassment to the United States, but that wasn't the only problem. The U.S. had plenty of engineers who knew about rockets, but the government was hesitant to let them contribute to the space race.

During World War II, Nazi Germany had terrorized England with its V-2 rockets, and German rocket engineers had even planned a rocket that could reach New York City. However, the war ended before the engineers could complete the design. After the war, the U.S. government recognized the value of the German rocket scientists and invited them to live and work in the United States.

By 1957, about 100 of the German rocket engineers were working for the United States Army. The team was led by Wernher von Braun, who had previously directed the V-2 rocket program in Germany.

Thanks to the help of von Braun and his team, the U.S. Army was able to build a rocket powerful enough to launch a satellite. Given the chance, the rocket probably could have launched a satellite before *Sputnik*. However, President Dwight D. Eisenhower, a former WWII general, thought that using a military rocket for a scientific mission would be a diplomatic mistake. In addition, he believed that using a rocket designed by engineers who had once built rockets used to bomb

U.S. allies would be even worse. Instead, Eisenhower asked the U.S. Naval Research Laboratory to speed up the development of the Viking rocket it was designing.

First, Failure

Even though the Viking rocket needed more work, the U.S. government pushed ahead with its plans to launch a satellite. On December 6, 1957, just a month after the second *Sputnik* launch, the Viking stood on the launchpad ready for countdown. Its "passenger" was *Vanguard*, a tiny, 6-inch (15-centimeters) sphere. When the moment for liftoff came, Viking roared, rose a few inches above the launchpad, and then, in one disastrous moment, collapsed to the ground.

In their book, *Moonshot: The Inside Story of America's Race to the Moon*, astronauts Alan Shepard and Deke Slayton remember that moment vividly. They say the rocket "spat fire, rocked, lurched forward, and fell back, breaking apart and crumpling into a ghastly fireball that seared the eyes of America."

The little *Vanguard* satellite fell off the top of the rocket and rolled into the shrubs. A few moments later, it began beeping the radio signals it should have been sending back from space. It was not a good beginning.

Waiting in the Wings

Meanwhile, von Braun and his team had been waiting in the wings. They knew this was their opportunity to do something positive with rockets. They quickly modified an Army four-stage rocket called Jupiter C (named after the Roman king of the gods) and gave it a new, gentler name—Juno 1 (in honor of Jupiter's wife).

Wernher von Braun: Rocket Genius

Wernher von Braun grew up in Germany. As a boy, he dreamed of building rockets that could fly to the Moon. Before he was 10 years old, he was building small test rockets. One early misfire sent the produce at a neighborhood fruit stand flying in all directions.

When von Braun was 18 years old, he joined a group of young men interested in building rockets. Using scrap materials, the group built and launched some eighty-five rockets—including one that could shoot 1 mile (1.6 km) into the air.

In 1932, the German army asked von Braun and some of his friends to design rockets for military purposes. This seemed like a perfect opportunity—at last the group would have the money they needed to do their rocket research.

At the time, Germany was not at war. However, Adolf Hitler was just coming to power, and he had big plans for Germany— plans that eventually led to World War II. The rocket builders later claimed that, initially, they didn't know that the army planned to use the rockets to carry weapons.

Eventually, of course, von Braun and his colleagues learned how the rockets would be used. This group of men was responsible for developing the notorious V-2 rockets that killed and terrified thousands of civilians in Great Britain and continental Europe in 1944 and 1945.

Through a strange twist of fate, von Braun and nearly 100 of his colleagues from Germany ended up coming to the United States—a country they had been at war with just a few years earlier. Under von Braun's expert leadership, the rocket scientists went to work for NASA. Using their V-2 design as a model, the German scientists eventually built many rockets—including the big Saturn 5 rocket that sent Americans to the Moon. Von Braun's passion for space and dedication to excellence paid off for NASA and provided a strong start for the U. S. presence in space in the 1950s, 1960s, and 1970s.

Wernher von Braun headed the rocket team that sent the first U.S. satellite *Explorer 1*—and many other successful missions—into space.

At the same time, a team of engineers at the Jet Propulsion Laboratory (JPL) in Pasadena, California, were building a satellite called *Explorer 1.* It measured just less than 7 feet (2 meters) long and 6 inches (15.2 cm) in diameter. It was larger than the Vanguard satellite but much smaller than the *Sputniks.* James Van Allen, a professor at the University of Iowa, designed a series of scientific experiments that fit inside *Explorer 1.*

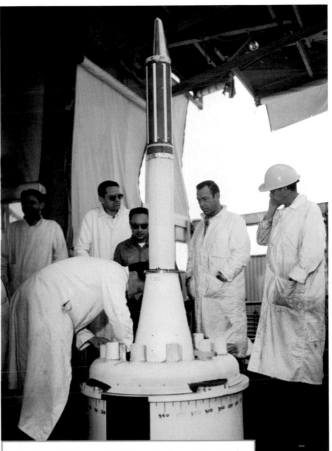

Explorer 1, the first U.S. satellite, was nearly 7 feet (2 m) long and about 6 inches (15.2 cm) wide and looked a lot like a stovepipe.

On January 31, 1958, Juno 1 carried *Explorer 1* into Earth-orbit. As it soared into space, the satellite collected scientific information about cosmic rays, micrometeorites, and atmospheric temperature. *Explorer 1* sent back news that a belt of radiation lies 600 to 3,000 miles (1,000 to 5,000 kilometer) above Earth's equator. This region, now known as the inner Van Allen Belt, was named after the scientist who designed the equipment used to detect it. The United States finally had a presence in space.

The Beginning of NASA

The thrill of success soon faded, however. During the next month, the United States faced some setbacks. The second Viking launch failed, and an attempt to launch *Explorer 2* with another Juno rocket also fizzled. The first successful *Vanguard* satellite finally soared into space on March 17, 1958.

The Soviet Union's *Sputnik 3* followed in May. By now, the world's attention was riveted on space. It was clear that the United States needed to take a bold, strong position in the arena of space technology.

To pave the way, President Eisenhower signed the National Aeronautics and Space Act of 1958. The act created the National Aeronautics and Space Administration (NASA). Replacing the former National Advisory Committee for Aeronautics (NACA), NASA opened for business on October 1, 1958.

Less than 3 months later, on December 17, 1958, NASA announced that it would develop a piloted satellite program. The Mercury program would send Americans into space for the first time.

Chapter 2

Americans Zoom into Space

NASA scientists and engineers faced a huge challenge. They had to figure out how to get humans into space. Would they try to develop a rocket plane or would they shoot astronauts into space atop a rocket? What kind of spacecraft would the astronauts travel in? How would they survive in space—a place that is extremely cold and has no oxygen, no air pressure, and no gravity. And, finally, how would the astronauts return to Earth?

Choosing Astronauts

Perhaps the most important question was who would make the first dangerous, but incredibly exciting journey into space? By February 1959, the selection process for astronauts was well underway.

When Wally Schirra received an order to report to the Pentagon, he did so "with no inkling why." When he arrived, he learned that he was one of 110 military test pilots selected as potential astronauts. NASA officials had decided that test pilots would make good astronauts. After all, they risked their lives during every flight and were trained to function well under stress. In addition, their understanding of experimental aircraft would come in handy when it came time to pilot a spacecraft. Because the spacecraft they would be in was small, no one taller than 5 feet 11 inches (182 cm) was selected.

In April 1959, 7 of the 110 pilots were chosen to become astronauts. The group became known as the "Mercury Seven," and their names would become famous: M. Scott Carpenter, L. Gordon Cooper Jr., John H. Glenn Jr., Virgil I. "Gus" Grissom, Walter "Wally" Schirra Jr., Alan B. Shepard Jr., and Donald K. "Deke" Slayton.

"Spam in a Can"

By the time the first astronauts were chosen, dozens of NASA scientists and engineers were hard at work designing spacecraft and propulsion systems. NASA and the U.S. Air Force spent a great deal of time and money developing and testing rocket-powered airplanes. However, they eventually decided that building a winged aircraft that could survive the heat of re-entry would present too many design challenges. As a result, they opted for a rocket-plus-spacecraft combination.

The "Mercury Seven": Front row, left to right, Walter M. "Wally" Schirra Jr., Donald K. "Deke" Slayton, John H. Glenn, Jr., and M. Scott Carpenter. Back row, left to right, Alan B. Shepard Jr., Virgil I. "Gus" Grissom, and L. Gordon Cooper Jr.

At the same time, other people at NASA were working on equipment that would protect astronauts from the extreme conditions of space. The astronauts would need special spacesuits, helmets, visors, life support systems, and other equipment to endure very high and very low temperatures, an airless environment, and radiation. The new spacecraft also had to provide a method for reentering Earth's atmosphere.

The Mercury capsule was barely big enough for one astronaut.

In many cases, the astronauts were directly involved in checking the design and production quality of the spacecraft. As Wally Schirra wrote in his book *Schirra's Space*, "My most beautiful memory of the Mercury Program is how seven men—all superachievers with super egos—came together to work as a team. We had total faith in one another . . . ."

From the beginning, the Mercury spacecraft was referred to as a capsule. It was a tiny, bell-shaped cabin, barely big enough for one pilot. The astronauts traveled on their backs, squeezed into the wide end of the bell. Among their jet pilot friends, the Mercury capsule earned the nickname "man in a can," which later turned up in the newspapers as "Spam in a can."

Each astronaut's seat was custom-molded to make sure that the heavy backward pressure of *liftoff* was evenly distributed over the astronaut's entire body. A porthole on one side of the capsule and a periscope overhead provided a very limited view outside the spacecraft.

The outside walls of the capsule were constructed of nickel alloy with an outer skin of heat-resistant titanium. A heat shield at the base of the bell provided protection from the intense heat that would occur when the spacecraft reentered Earth's atmosphere at speeds up to 15,000 miles (24,135 km) per hour.

An escape tower perched above the capsule during liftoff. If the rocket malfunctioned, this tower would pull the capsule and its pilot out of danger. Luckily, this feature was never used, except during testing.

By December 1960, many tests had been made. One involved an unpiloted Mercury capsule, which was successfully recovered from a *suborbital* flight—a flight into space that does not achieve sufficient altitude to orbit Earth. NASA had checked every aspect of the program—escape systems, controls, heat protection on reentry, aerodynamics, and recovery. They used test monkeys and simulated human pilots to verify the safety of liftoff and ascent, suborbital flight, and descent.

Another test followed in January 1961. This one carried a passenger—a chimpanzee named Ham. The test went well, and Ham returned to Earth in excellent health. The Mercury program was almost ready to send a human into space. But once again the United States was beaten in the space race by the Soviet Union.

"I am an ordinary Soviet man," Yuri Gagarin once said. Gagarin was an unassuming test pilot, a charming man who seemed genuinely humble, but his place in history is anything but ordinary. He was the first human ever to enter space and the first to orbit Earth. On April

Yuri Gagarin and Valentina Tereshkova, both of the Soviet Union, were the first man (April 1961) and woman (June 1963) in space. Both became international heroes.

12, 1961, he circled the planet for nearly an hour and a half (89.5 minutes). The Soviet mission made worldwide headlines and Gagarin became an international hero. The United States took the news badly.

The First U.S. Space Heroes

Wanting to be sure that the first Mercury flight would be flawless and present minimal risk to the astronaut, NASA tested and retested the equipment. Even though Ham had fared well on his flight, von Braun was concerned about some problems in the Redstone rocket that would be used to propel the Mercury capsule.

He had insisted on another test in March before he would okay the project for human flight. The test in March had gone well, and some people have pointed out that if NASA had sent an astronaut up at that time, the United States would have been the first nation to put a human in space.

Now the United States was behind again. Once again, the Soviet Union had built a fire under the U.S. space program. Within 23 days of the Gagarin flight, astronaut Alan Shepard was sitting on the launchpad at Cape Canaveral, Florida, waiting for the countdown.* He was about to become America's first space hero.

On the morning of May 5, 1961, Shepard crawled into the tiny, 9.5-foot (3-m)-tall space capsule. He had named it *Freedom 7*. Finally, 4 hours later, after many delays, clouds of oxygen vapor engulfed the big, white Redstone rocket. The countdown reached liftoff, and the rocket and its cargo lifted skyward. From inside came Shepard's voice, calm and almost casual: "Ahh, Roger; liftoff and the clock has started . . . Yes, sir, reading you loud and clear. This is *Freedom 7*."

The tremendous force of liftoff pressed Shepard heavily into his custom-fitted seat. The rocket sped to 5,180 miles (8,335 km) per hour. Then, at an altitude of 116.5 miles (187 km) above Earth's surface, the engines cut off and the rocket dropped away. The astronaut and spacecraft were on their own, hurtling through space at four times the speed of sound.

Shepard tested the controls, which he found worked smoothly, and that was about all he had time for. Within minutes, *Freedom 7*

* Cape Canaveral was called Cape Kennedy from 1963 to 1973. This Air Force launch station is still used by NASA and the military as well as commercial and international clients.

The small, black object at the top of this powerful rocket is the Mercury capsule.

automatically moved into position for return to Earth. With its bottom downward and the heat shield in place, the little spacecraft fired its three retro-rockets to slow the capsule's speed.

At 21,000 feet (6,400 m) above Earth, a small parachute opened to steady the fall, followed by the main parachute to put on the brakes. The little spacecraft, with Alan Shepard inside, plunged into the Atlantic Ocean. It landed just 40 miles (64 km) from the planned tar-

Science at Work: What Happens to Humans in Zero-G?

Before the first human traveled into space, no one was sure exactly how the human body would react in zero gravity (zero-g). Plant and animal life on Earth has always been subject to the planet's constant gravitational pull. What would happen to human circulatory and respiratory systems without gravity? Would our muscles work? Would we be able to think without that familiar tug on our brain cells? When space flights became longer, scientists also had to worry about the astronauts' digestive systems, cardiovascular systems, and bones.

Humans were not the first creatures sent into space. When test animals traveled beyond Earth's atmosphere, they were hooked up to a variety of electrodes and sensors that measured their bodily functions. These animals experienced no major problems, and neither did the astronauts that followed them. Studies of the extended effects of zero gravity continue today.

get. Within minutes, Shepard was safely aboard the recovery ship. It was definitely a whirlwind trip—only 25 minutes had passed since liftoff, and the flight itself had taken only 15 minutes and 22 seconds.

Yuri Gagarin's flight seemed more ambitious. He had achieved orbit and stayed in space for 108 minutes, but, unlike Shepard, Gargarin did not have control of his spacecraft. President John F. Kennedy was impressed by the success of Shepard's flight and telephoned his congratulations to the triumphant astronaut.

In his famous speech on May 25, 1961—less than a month after Shepard's flight—Kennedy announced, "I believe that this nation should commit itself to achieving the goal, before this decade is out, of landing a man on the moon and returning him safely to the earth."

Kennedy had captured the mood of the nation. Congress did not object to the giant undertaking, and newspapers and magazines endorsed it heartily. The United States was headed for the Moon.

A Close Call

In July 1961, Gus Grissom took the second Mercury spacecraft, *Liberty Bell 7*, into suborbital flight. His flight lasted only a bit longer than Shepard's, but it ended in a close call. As *Liberty Bell 7* bobbed about in the Atlantic Ocean waiting to be picked up, the escape hatch suddenly blew off and the spacecraft began taking on water. Grissom dived out, into the cold water, and bobbed there until a Marine Corps helicopter was able to pick him up. Unfortunately, *Liberty Bell 7* sank to the ocean floor. The water it had taken on made it too heavy for the helicopter to pull it out.

A U.S. Marine Corps helicopter tries to lift Gus Grissom's *Liberty Bell 7* Mercury spacecraft from the Atlantic Ocean. Grissom was picked up, but his spacecraft sank.

Going Orbital

The U.S. astronauts still had not made an orbital flight. The Redstone rockets that propelled the first two Mercury capsules were not powerful enough to carry the spacecraft into orbit. Wernher von Braun and his team were busy testing a *ballistic missile* named Atlas for the job.

Finally, the Atlas was ready. The most experienced pilot, John Glenn, had been chosen to travel in the spacecraft he called *Friendship 7*. On February 20, 1962, the Atlas rocket lifted off. Traveling 17,500 miles (28,100 km) per hour, Glenn quickly reached orbit and began the first of three revolutions around Earth. As he looked toward his

As the end of the countdown drew near, John Glenn climbed into the *Friendship 7* spacecraft. He was about to become the first U.S. astronaut to orbit Earth.

home planet, Glenn was struck by Earth's beauty. He saw piles of clouds swirling through the atmosphere, dust storms in Africa, and a sensational sunset.

"Orbital sunset is tremendous . . . a truly beautiful, beautiful sight," he said. "As the sun goes down a little bit more, the bottom layer becomes orange, and it fades into red, and finally off into blues and black as you look farther up into space."

On the ground, controllers worried. Early in the flight, they had noticed that the spacecraft's heat shield seemed to be loose. That heat shield was essential to Glenn's safety. Without it, he would be burned to a crisp, just as most *meteoroids* are when they enter Earth's atmosphere. The ground controllers told Glenn to keep the retro-rockets in place after they fired at the end of his flight, even though they were usually jettisoned. Maybe they would hold the heat shield in place.

As it turned out, though, the heat shield was intact, and John Glenn splashed down aboard *Friendship 7* with no problems. His flight had lasted a long 4 hours, 55 minutes, and 23 seconds. Glenn was treated to a hero's welcome, including a ticker-tape parade in New York City. His successful flight made newspaper headlines all over the world, and the United States regained some of its lost prestige in the space race.

Final Voyages

Three months later, Scott Carpenter orbited Earth three times aboard *Aurora 7*. At one point, Carpenter became so entranced with the view that he briefly lost control of the spacecraft. As a result, he landed 250 miles (402 km) from the arranged pickup point. Recovery ships had to scramble to reach him.

Mercury Mission Facts

Vital Statistics

Spacecraft	Date of Splashdown	Astronaut	Highlights
MERCURY 2	January 31, 1961	Ham, a chimpanzee	Ham is the first passenger on a sub-orbital Mercury flight that lasts 16.5 minutes.
FREEDOM 7	May 5, 1961	Alan Shepard	Shepard is the first American in space. His sub-orbital flight lasts 15 minutes and 22 seconds.
LIBERTY BELL 7	July 21, 1961	Gus Grissom	Suborbital flight that lasts 16 minutes
MERCURY 5	November 29, 1961	Enos, a chimpanzee	Enos is the first passenger on an orbital Mercury flight. The spacecraft orbits Earth twice.
FRIENDSHIP 7	February 20, 1962	John Glenn	The first American orbital flight orbits Earth three times and lasts almost 5 hours.
AURORA 7	May 24, 1962	Scott Carpenter	3 orbits; 4.9 hours
SIGMA 7	October 3, 1962	Willy Schirra	6 orbits; 9.25 hours
FAITH 7	May 15, 1963	Gordon Cooper	22.5 orbits; 34.3 hours

The remaining two Mercury flights—Wally Schirra's in October 1962 and Gordon Cooper's in May 1963—went smoothly. The Mercury program had proved a successful first step in NASA's effort to reach the Moon. By mid-1963, only 500 of the 2,500 people at NASA's Manned Spacecraft Center in Houston, Texas, were still working on Mercury. The rest were focusing their attention on the Gemini and the Apollo programs, the next steps toward reaching the Moon.

Chapter 3

Walking and Docking in Space

Now, a new, bigger, and better spacecraft came off the production line. It was called "Gemini" (Latin for "twins") because the spacecraft was big enough for a crew of two. Astronaut Buzz Aldrin would later recall, ". . . Gemini was a true spacecraft, meant to voyage in space, not simply to penetrate the new environment like the Mercury capsule." The main purpose of the Gemini program was to prove that two spacecraft could meet and dock in space. This maneuver would be essential during Apollo missions to the Moon.

Walking in Space

The first crewed Gemini spacecraft lifted off in March 1965. Astronauts Gus Grissom and John Young were on board. The spacecraft orbited Earth three times.* The mission went well and *Gemini 3* splashed down successfully.

Gemini 3 heads for space atop the powerful Titan rocket (left). Grissom and Young orbited Earth three times and splashed down successfully 5 hours after liftoff. Their capsule was pulled out of the water without mishap (right).

---

* Grissom jokingly named the *Gemini 3* spacecraft *Molly Brown* after the popular Broadway musical *The Unsinkable Molly Brown*. NASA officials didn't like the apparent reference to Grissom's last (more sinkable) spacecraft, which had ended up on the ocean floor. However, authorities preferred that to his second choice, *Titanic*.

Meanwhile, the Soviets embarrassed NASA again. Alexei Leonov, an athletic young *cosmonaut*, made the first space walk in history on March 18, 1965—just 5 days before Grissom and Young's mission was launched. NASA was planning a space walk, but it was scheduled for the crew of *Gemini 4*. Now, the pressure was really on.

Astronaut Ed White was chosen for the daunting challenge. The Soviets kept the details of Leonov's space walk secret, so NASA and its astronauts were on their own. For the first time, a U.S. astronaut would venture out of the safety of the spacecraft and into the harsh environment of space with only a spacesuit and an oxygen hose for life support and protection. NASA used an unwieldy name—*extravehicular activity* or, more simply, EVA—to describe this adventure.

On Earth, we live at the bottom of a deep layer of atmosphere, and our bodies are adapted to the presence of air and air pressure. In the vacuum of space, however, there is no atmosphere and no atmospheric pressure. We couldn't live, even for a moment, without a pressurized suit or spacecraft to protect our body organs from bursting. That's one reason an EVA is so dangerous. EVAs are also difficult because the bulk of a spacesuit, space gloves, and helmet is clumsy. Moving around in the weightlessness of space is awkward and difficult to adapt to—a little like floating in water, but without the resistance that water provides.

The special pressurized suit and other equipment required for a full EVA were not ready until May 19—just 6 days before *Gemini 4*'s planned launch date. Until then, NASA officials weren't sure whether the space walk would really take place. White was ready, though. He had been preparing for months in a high-altitude pressure chamber in St. Louis, Missouri.

Finally, on June 3, the launch took place, with Jim McDivitt as the pilot. This was the first mission directed after liftoff from the Manned Spacecraft Center in Texas. Previously, all missions had been managed from Cape Kennedy in Florida.

The mission plan called for a *rendezvous* with the emptied second stage of the Titan rocket that had launched them, but that didn't go well. The crew decided to abandon that part of their mission and moved on to their most important task. On the third orbit, the astronauts partially depressurized the cabin and tested their spacesuit pressure.

McDivitt and White were both nervous. McDivitt grabbed at the spacecraft's hatch to keep it from opening too far. He knew that if the hatch jammed, they would never make it back to Earth alive. Meanwhile, White prepared to exit. He checked his camera three times, worried that he might forget to remove the lens cap. "I knew I might as well not come back if I did," he joked later.

He also had to put together a little rocket gun, a handheld unit that blew puffs of gas wherever it was pointed. White could use this little rocket to move about outside. He also had a tether he could use to change his position. "Changing my position by pulling on the tether was easy," he later remarked, "like pulling a trout, say a 2- or 3-pounder, out of a stream on a light line."

Finally, after 12 minutes of preparation with the hatch open, the first American EVA began. Ed White floated out the hatch into the airlessness of space. A long connecting hose extended like an umbilical cord from White to the Gemini spacecraft. This gold-colored hose covered with mylar passed oxygen, communications, and power to the astronaut.

White had some difficulty controlling his movements outside the spacecraft. Once he started in one direction, it was hard to put on the

Ed White floated high above Earth's clouds during the first U.S. EVA.

brakes. He had trouble avoiding the spacecraft. Meanwhile, inside, McDivitt found it difficult to control the spacecraft with White outside pulling on the umbilical cord and tether. Despite these difficulties, White enjoyed the spectacular view.

As Earth floated below him, White reported to McDivitt and the ground crew, "I can sit out here and see the whole California coast." He was traveling at a speed of 17,500 miles (28,100 km) per hour.

After the adventure was over, White recalled, "Looking down, I could see all the lower part of [Florida], the island chain of Cuba, and Puerto Rico." White spent a total of 21 minutes walking in space. His EVA had lasted twice as long as Leonov's.

From inside *Gemini 4*, McDivitt and White also saw traffic lights, roads, and other details on Earth's surface. They took magnificent pictures and studied weather systems. The 4-day flight was the longest yet made by American astronauts.

The next Gemini crew doubled McDivitt and White's time in space. Gordon Cooper and Charles "Pete" Conrad spent 8 days aboard *Gemini 5*. This crew released the first satellite launched from a spacecraft.

The following two missions, *Gemini 6-A* and *Gemini 7*, orbited at the same time and met up with each other in space. Walter Schirra skillfully steered *Gemini 6-A* within 6 feet (2 m) of *Gemini 7* and hovered there for 5½ hours. The *Gemini 7* spacecraft spent 2 weeks in space, setting an international record for the longest space flight. The record stood unbroken for 5 years.

Meeting Up in Space

The next challenge was docking. Neil Armstrong and David Scott's mission aboard *Gemini 8* was designed to show that the Gemini spacecraft could be docked with a crewless spacecraft called the *Agena*. The two spacecraft were launched separately on the same day. Six hours

Gemini 8's *Agena* docking target orbited high above Earth's surface. Learning to rendezvous and dock spacecraft prepared the astronauts, and NASA, for future trips to the Moon.

after launch, *Gemini 8* pulled up to the *Agena* and hovered 24 inches (61 cm) away. Tension was high in the little cabin as Armstrong eased his spacecraft slowly into the *docking adapter*. Moments later, the latches snapped into place and the two spacecraft were joined. Everything had gone smoothly.

Or had it? Suddenly the two spacecraft began to buck. What if the docking assembly broke? The crew quickly detached their spacecraft from the *Agena* and backed away, but the bucking didn't stop. Something on board the *Gemini* spacecraft was malfunctioning. But what? Finally, the astronauts realized that one of their rocket thrusters was firing out of control, and shut it down. Almost 75 percent of their fuel had been wasted. They had to abandon the rest of their mission, but they had succeeded in docking in space.

Gemini Mission Facts

Vital Statistics

Spacecraft	Date of Launch	Astronaut	Highlights
GEMINI 1	April 8, 1964	None	Crewless test flight that orbits for 4 days
GEMINI 2	January 19, 1965	None	18-minute suborbital test of the heat shield
GEMINI 3 "MOLLY BROWN"	March 23, 1965	Gus Grissom John Young	First truly piloted spacecraft flight
GEMINI 4	June 3, 1965	Ed White James McDivitt	62 orbits; 4-day flight; White makes first U.S. EVA
GEMINI 5	August 21, 1965	Gordon Cooper Pete Conrad	120 orbits; 8-day flight
GEMINI 7	December 4, 1965	Frank Borman Jim Lovell	14-day flight sets international duration record that is not broken for 5 years; rendezvous with *Gemini 6-A*
GEMINI 6-A	December 15, 1965	Wally Schirra Tom Stafford	Rendezvous with *Gemini 7*, within a few feet
GEMINI 8	March 16, 1966	Neil Armstrong Dave Scott	First docking of two spacecraft; *Gemini 8* links up with crewless *Agena* target vehicle; the linked spacecraft spins out of control, but makes a safe emergency landing

Vital Statistics

Spacecraft	Date of Launch	Astronaut	Highlights
GEMINI 9-A	June 3, 1966	Tom Stafford Eugene Cernan	Cernan makes a 2-hour EVA
GEMINI 10	July 18, 1966	Mike Collins John Young	EVAs by Collins; two rendezvous and docking maneuvers with *Agena*
GEMINI 11	September 12, 1966	Pete Conrad Richard Gordon	Two EVAs; a high orbit of 850 miles (1,367 km) is achieved while docked with the *Agena*; artificial gravity experiment
GEMINI 12	November 11, 1966	Jim Lovell Buzz Aldrin	Three EVAs (the first truly successful ones); docking with *Agena*; artificial-gravity experiments; fully automated reentry

EVA: Not a Piece of Cake

On February 28, 1966, the original *Gemini 9* crew, Elliott See and Charles Bassett, died in a tragic plane crash. Their mission was flown instead (under the name *Gemini 9-A*) by backup crew Tom Stafford and Eugene Cernan on June 3, 1966.

During that mission, Cernan broke all EVA records with a 2-hour space walk, but he ran into serious difficulties. Part of his mission involved testing a backpack propulsion system. As he struggled to put on the backpack, his pulse rate climbed dangerously high and he became overheated. In addition, his visor fogged up so badly that he couldn't see. Later, Dick Gordon, a member of the *Gemini 11* crew, would also become blinded by sweat during his EVA as he tried to attach a tether to the *Agena* spacecraft.

As a result of these problems, NASA engineers tried to resolve some of the difficulties that made weightlessness so frustrating and exertion so extreme. By now, NASA engineers were famous for solving critical problems with ingenious, practical solutions. The EVA problems were no exception.

When Jim Lovell and Buzz Aldrin flew *Gemini 12*, they took along an array of specially designed gadgets. During his EVA, Aldrin became the first astronaut-mechanic. He installed an exterior handrail that he could hook up to by using nylon tethers attached to his spacesuit. He also attached portable Velcro handholds to the exterior of *Agena*. At a workshop area on *Agena*, he clamped into a specially designed restraint for his feet. This freed his hands to do other jobs. Aldrin showed that, even weightless, he could screw and unscrew bolts and manipulate connectors. NASA was getting a handle on the difficulties of EVA.

The final three Gemini missions—*Gemini 10, Gemini 11*, and *Gemini 12*—completed most of the rest of the ambitious goals set out for Project Gemini. The astronauts performed each rendezvous smoothly and docked with their *Agena* targets efficiently. They even moved the combined spacecraft to a different orbit.

The Gemini program ended when Aldrin and Lovell splashed down aboard *Gemini 12* on November 15, 1966. American astronauts had added nearly 2,000 hours to their time in space. The Gemini flights had been real workhorses and had laid the groundwork for the future NASA missions. Ahead lay Apollo and the Moon.

Chapter 4

Heading for the Moon

While the Gemini crews were walking in space, making rendezvous, and docking spacecraft, many scientists and engineers at NASA were working more directly on the journey to the Moon. Some were building and testing a rocket that could send a spacecraft all the way to the Moon. Others were designing the complex spacecraft that would carry astronauts to the Moon, land them on the lunar surface, and safely return them to Earth. Still others were choosing landing sites or developing new equipment for the astronauts.

The astronauts were hard at work, too. They had to be prepared for their incredible journey. Everyone working on the program recognized that a voyage to the Moon was a tremendous and taxing undertaking that would require hard work, dedication, and tremendous attention to detail.

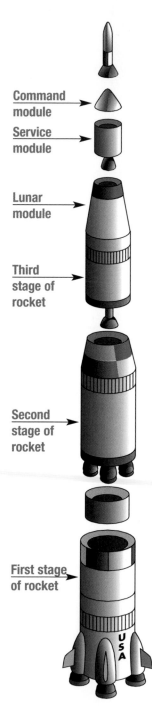

Command module

Service module

Lunar module

Third stage of rocket

Second stage of rocket

First stage of rocket

Powering Up: The Saturn 5 Rocket

Wernher von Braun's team at the Marshall Space Flight Center in Huntsville, Alabama, was in charge of developing NASA's rockets. In the early 1960s, they began work on a huge *multistage, liquid-fuel rocket* called Saturn 5 that would make earlier rockets look like a child's toy.

A multistage rocket is actually a group of rockets. The Saturn 5 rocket consisted of three stages. The first two stages—called the *boosters*—launched the rocket and started it on its way. They had to be large enough to over-come the force of gravity and also lift the rocket's upper stages and the Apollo spacecraft. When each booster used up its fuel, it separated and fell away and the next stage fired up. The third stage put the spacecraft into orbit around Earth and then on course to the Moon.

The enormous Saturn 5 rocket was far more powerful than the rockets that launched the Mercury and Gemini missions. Atop its three stages rode the three-part spacecraft that made up Apollo: The lunar module that would land on the Moon, the service module with its power and support systems, and the command module that ferried the astronauts to and from the Moon.

A multistage rocket also has another advantage—its speed is cumulative. For example, if the top speed of each stage of a three-stage rocket is 100 miles (161 km) per hour, the whole rocket will be traveling 100 miles (161 km) per hour when the first stage drops away and the second stage starts. If the second stage were launched from a standing start, its maximum potential speed would be also 100 miles (161 km) per hour. But since the spacecraft is already going 100 miles (161 km) per hour, the top speed of the second stage is 200 miles (322 km) per hour. When the third stage starts, it adds its 100-mile (161-km)-per-hour speed to the rocket's 200-mile (322-km)-per-hour speed, so the rocket's final maximum velocity is 300 miles (483 km) per hour.

As early as 1912, rocket scientists realized that liquid fuels are the best choice for rockets. They are more powerful than *solid fuels* and they can be controlled. Once a solid-fuel rocket, such as a rocket powered by gunpowder, is started, it cannot be stopped. However, the fuel and the *oxidizer* needed to power a liquid-fuel rocket are stored in separate containers, so it is possible to stop a liquid-fuel rocket by blocking the flow of fuel to the engine where it comes into contact with the oxidizer.

To restart a liquid-fuel rocket, all you have to do is restore the flow of fuel into the engine. To control the rocket's speed, you simply adjust the rate at which the fuel and oxidizer flow into the engine.

Designing the Apollo Spacecraft

In the meantime, intense work had begun on the three-part spacecraft that would carry the three-member crews to Earth orbit and then on to the Moon, where they would orbit and land. The service module (SM) would carry fuel, provisions, and the spacecraft's engines.

Astronauts Frank Borman, James A. Lovell Jr., and William A. Anders training inside the Apollo command module

The command module (CM) was the main traveling cabin from Earth to the Moon and back.

Once the Apollo spacecraft reached orbit around the Moon, two of the three crew members would enter the much smaller lunar module (LM). Then this mini-spacecraft would separate from the other two parts of the Apollo spacecraft and descend to the Moon's surface. There, the two-person exploration team would walk on the surface of the Moon.

When the visit to the Moon was over, the LM would use a propulsion system to lift off. Once the astronauts had returned to the combined command and service modules (CSM), they would dock and reenter the command module. There, they would rejoin their pilot and head back home to Earth.

Apollo 1: Trapped in Flames

The Apollo spacecraft design process did not go smoothly. As a joke, Gus Grissom hung a lemon outside the command module. The joke turned out to hold a bitter kind of truth.

On January 27, 1967, Grissom, Ed White, and Roger Chaffee—the designated crew for the *Apollo 1* mission—boarded the spacecraft for a ground test of the equipment. Moments later, a fire broke out inside the capsule. On the outside, technicians struggled to open the hatch, but they were too late. The pure-oxygen environment caused the flames to ignite the whole interior almost instantly, and the three astronauts couldn't get out before they became asphyxiated. All three astronauts died.

NASA and the Apollo program became frozen in the wake of the tragedy. It took a year and a full redesign of the command module before even unpiloted tests were resumed.

Selecting a Landing Site: Surveying the Moon

Long before anyone set foot on the Moon, NASA had to know all about its surface. Had meteoroid impacts ground it to such a fine powder over billions of years that astronauts might sink up to their waists—or even over their heads—in the powdery dust? How rugged was the terrain? Could a spacecraft land there?

NASA began sending missions to the Moon very early. In fact, the first flyby, *Pioneer 4*, was launched in March 1959. In September, the first Soviet Probe landed on the Moon. By 1964, the United States obtained the world's first television pictures of the Moon, followed by numerous site surveys and soft landings on the Moon.

Scouting the Route: *Apollo 7* to *10*

Once the program began launching again, the first four piloted Apollo missions tested the equipment. Each mission answered a question. Wally Schirra, Donn Eisele, and Walter Cunningham flew *Apollo 7* in Earth orbit to test the command module.

Apollo 8 was the first piloted mission launched by the big Saturn 5 rocket. It was also the first spacecraft in history to carry human beings beyond Earth orbit and around another world. For a frightening few minutes, when astronauts Jim Lovell, Frank Borman, and William Anders were behind the Moon, they lost contact with NASA. Moments before communications went down, Lovell was casual. "We'll see you on the other side," he said. His message traveled across

Splashdown for *Apollo 7* was a smooth ending to a successful trial run in Earth orbit.

The *Apollo 9* lunar module named "Spider"

200,000 miles (321,860 km) of empty space to anxious listeners on Earth. When contact was restored, Lovell's voice came through loud and clear: "Go ahead, Houston, *Apollo 8*." The crew was safe, and the spacecraft was on its way home.

Apollo 9 ran more tests in Earth orbit. James McDivitt, David Scott, and Russell Schweickart had the job of making sure the lunar module would work in space. "Rusty" Schweickart and Jim McDivitt took the little LM called "Spider" out for a couple of spins, tested the hatch, and performed EVAs. The mission was a complete success.

Finally, the Apollo program was ready for a full dress rehearsal. After arriving in orbit around the Moon, *Apollo 10* astronauts Tom Stafford and Eugene Cernan took the LM called "Snoopy" out for a ride. They descended toward the Moon, but they stayed close enough to the CSM that pilot John Young could reach them if they had an emergency.

The astronauts were fascinated by the Moon's surface. They took a look at the Sea of Tranquillity, where *Apollo 11* would land, and reported that it was smooth with only a few pockmarks and a scattering of shallow craters. Things were looking good. The two astronauts returned to the command module and *Apollo 10* returned safely home.

The Giant Leap

At last, everything was ready. *Apollo 11* lifted off from Kennedy Space Center in Florida on July 16, 1969. Four days later, on July 20, the *Apollo 11* command module "Columbia" poised above the Moon as the lunar module called "Eagle" descended toward the Moon's surface. It was the historic moment John F. Kennedy had envisioned only 8 years earlier.

A lot had happened since then. Kennedy had met an early death at the hands of an assassin in Dallas, Texas. Vice President Lyndon Johnson had stepped in to take over and had nurtured the space program. The United States had also become deeply involved in the Vietnam War. In January 1969, Richard Nixon became president.

On July 20, 1969, came the triumphant moment that Americans had been waiting for. Millions watched their television screens and listened as the astronauts' voices crackled across the miles from the Moon. The LM the "Eagle" eased away from the command module and descended toward the Moon. Much of the conversation was technical, but everyone understood what was happening when they heard the words: "Houston, Tranquility Base here. The 'Eagle' has landed." As Neil Armstrong stepped onto the Moon's surface, he said for all to hear, "That's one small step for [a] man, one giant leap for mankind."

During the first Moon landing, astronaut Neil Armstrong took this photograph of fellow-astronaut Buzz Aldrin climbing down a ladder onto the Moon's surface.

Neil Armstrong and Buzz Aldrin spent nearly 2 days on the Moon's surface and returned with 44 pounds (19.9 kg) of lunar material. Later, in a broadcast from *Apollo 11*, Aldrin tried to set the experience in a larger context with these words: "This has been far more than three men on a mission to the Moon; more still than the efforts of a government and industry team; more, even, than the efforts of one nation. We feel this stands as a symbol of the insatiable curiosity of all mankind to explore the unknown."

"Houston: We've Had a Problem": *Apollo 13*

The next mission to the Moon, *Apollo 12*, went smoothly. When *Apollo 13* lifted off on April 11, 1970, there was no reason to expect anything but another flawless mission. There's no such thing as an unlucky number, but *Apollo 13* did not go smoothly. About 56 hours into the mission, the bad news came in to Mission Control: "Houston," said astronaut Jim Lovell, "we've had a problem here."

They had nearly reached the Moon when an explosion in the service module caused a critical emergency. The crew lost all oxygen and power in the command and service modules and the rest of the mission had to be scrubbed. All three astronauts crawled into the lunar module, which they used as a kind of lifeboat. They passed behind the Moon, temporarily moving out of contact with Houston. Then, using a boost from the Moon's gravity, they headed back toward Earth. The three-person crew had to live for 4 days on provisions intended to feed two men for 2 days, but they made it home again. Jim Lovell, Fred Haise, and John Swigert landed safely on April 17, 1970.

NASA engineers and technicians worked around the clock at Mission Control to solve technical problems and help get the *Apollo 13* astronauts home safely.

Exploring the Moon

After Armstrong and Aldrin, ten more astronauts explored the surface of the Moon. Like Armstrong and Aldrin, the *Apollo 12* and *Apollo 14* astronauts traveled on the Moon on foot. Astronauts on board *Apollo 15*, *16*, and *17* were able to ride around in a Lunar Roving Vehicle— or lunar rover, for short. The rover made traveling across the Moon a lot easier. They used it to roll across the flat, hardened areas of volcanic rock and ash and to clamber around craters.

The astronauts on all these missions brought back samples of Moon rock, took photographs, examined landforms, and spent as

Apollo Mission Facts

Vital Statistics

Spacecraft	Dates	Astronauts	Highlights
APOLLO 7	October 11–12, 1968	Wally Schirra, Donn Eisele, Walter Cunningham	Test in Earth-orbit
APOLLO 8	December 21–27, 1968	Frank Borman, James Lovell, William Anders	First crewed flight around the Moon
APOLLO 9	March 3–13, 1969	James McDivitt, David Scott, Russell Schweickart	First test of the lunar module (LM) in Earth McDivitt and Schweickart take the LM out for a flight and then redock with the Command Module
APOLLO 10	May 18–26, 1969	Thomas Stafford, John Young, Eugene Cernan	Final test drive before landing on the Moon; Stafford and Cernan take the lunar module into orbit around the Moon
APOLLO 11	July 16–24, 1969	Neil Armstrong, Michael Collins, Edwin "Buzz" Aldrin	Armstrong and Aldrin land on the Moon; they bring back 44 pounds (19.9 kg) of lunar material
APOLLO 12	November 14–24, 1969	Charles "Pete" Conrad, Richard Gordon, Alan Bean	In two EVA walks, Conrad and Bean spend 15 hours, 32 minutes exploring the Moon's surface and collecting samples

Vital Statistics

Spacecraft	Dates	Astronauts	Highlights
APOLLO 13	April 11–17, 1970	Jim Lovell, John Swigert, Fred Haise	Due to an explosion in the spacecraft's service module (SM), *Apollo 13* astronauts do not land on the Moon; they fly around the Moon and back home to Earth
APOLLO 14	January 31– February 9, 1971	Alan Shepard, Stuart Roosa, Edgar Mitchell	Collect samples from the crater Fra Mauro; Shepard plays golf on the Moon's surface
APOLLO 15	July 26– August 7, 1971	David Scott, Alfred Worden, James Irwin	First mission to use the lunar rover for transportation
APOLLO 16	April 16–27, 1972	John Young, Thomas "Ken" Mattingly, Charles Duke	Conduct experiments on the Moon's surface; detect magnetism at Descartes crater; find a prism of glass (indicating intense heating in the past)
APOLLO 17	December 7–19, 1965	Eugene Cernan, Ron Evans, Harrison Schmitt	Civilian geologist Schmitt directs scientific activities during lunar EVAs

much time as they could hiking or roving across the Moon's dusty terrain. A civilian geologist named Harrison Schmitt added his scientific expertise to *Apollo 17*, the last mission to the Moon's surface.

The astronauts who participated in the *Apollo 15*, *16*, and *17* missions toured the Moon's surface aboard a lunar rover.

On December 19, 1972, *Apollo 17* returned home, and a great era of space exploration drew to a close. While NASA sent robot planetary missions to nearly every corner of the solar system in the years that followed, no spacecraft returned to the Moon until the 1990s, and, so far, no human crews have ever returned there. The footprints the astronauts left are still there, and they will remain there for thousands of years—as long as no one destroys them and no meteorites obliterate them.

Apollo's Other Accomplishments

The Apollo spacecraft did more than carry the first humans to the Moon. In 1975, in a rare Cold War gesture of peace and cooperation between the USSR and the United States, the two countries completed a joint mission. A Soviet Soyuz spacecraft docked with an Apollo spacecraft in Earth orbit, and the two crews crowded into the Apollo spacecraft to shake hands in an internationally televised gesture. Known as Apollo-Soyuz, the mission signaled the beginning of a thaw in the Cold War.

In addition, surplus Apollo hardware, Saturn booster rockets, and two segments of the Apollo spacecraft—the command module and the service module—were used to build the *Skylab* space station. The plan for creating the space station was economical, efficient, and productive, as well as adventurous.

NASA converted an empty, unused booster rocket into a two-level compartment with separate areas for living and working. This portion of *Skylab* was assembled and outfitted on Earth and lifted into orbit in May 1973 by a spare Saturn 5 rocket. The Soviets had built space stations, but no one had ever before put a space station this large into orbit. It was the size of a three-bedroom house, and on Earth it weighed nearly 3 tons.

From May 1973 to January 1974, three crews of astronauts worked aboard *Skylab* for periods of about 2 months each. They observed the reactions of living things, such as two spiders named Arabella and Anita. The spiders quickly learned to spin webs in the weightlessness of space. The astronauts also examined the effects of weightlessness on themselves, performed many EVAs, took dozens of photos of Earth from space, and studied the Sun. In

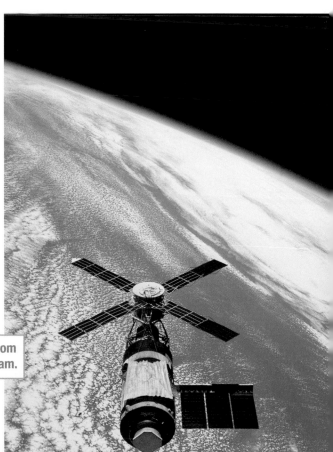

The *Skylab* space station was built from parts salvaged from the Apollo program.

the process, they added to scientific knowledge about our planet, the solar system, and working in space.

Originally, NASA had planned to keep *Skylab* in orbit by nudging it with its next planned launch program, the Space Shuttle. However, the Space Shuttle plans were delayed. Funding for space exploration dwindled because relations with the USSR had improved dramatically and because the United States was deeply involved in the Vietnam War. *Skylab* could not maintain its orbit without a nudge, and NASA had no way of giving it a push. On July 11, 1979, *Skylab* reentered Earth's atmosphere above the Indian Ocean, broke up, and scattered in pieces over uninhabited regions of Australia and the Pacific Ocean.

A Victory for the United States

Looking back, some critics have questioned the value of the Mercury, Gemini, and Apollo programs. Admittedly, President Kennedy's reasons were primarily political when he called on Americans to put so much effort into landing on the Moon. The United States needed to prove—to the world and to itself—that it could achieve such an impressive feat.

The legacy, though, reaches much farther than that. Before 1961, no one had ever left the safety of Earth's atmosphere. Before 1968, no one had ever ventured to any other body in the solar system. The United States proved that its people could develop the technology required to travel more than 200,000 miles (322,000 km) through space, land on another world, explore the surface of that world, and return safely to Earth. *Apollo 13* showed how resourceful NASA engineers could be in solving critical, life-threatening problems. The scientific and technological knowledge developed during the Mercury, Gemini, and Apollo programs is overwhelming.

Chapter 5

Exploring the Universe

Before the *Explorer 1* satellite's first voyage beyond Earth's atmosphere, humans knew very little about space. Scientists didn't even know about the radiation belts that encircle our own planet. Since those early days of space exploration, NASA has been gathering exciting information about the solar system with nearly every mission. It has sent robotic probes to almost every planet in the solar system and has placed a variety of observational satellites in Earth orbit. Each one is a part of NASA's primary goal—to expand our knowledge of the vast regions of space, the physical laws that make things work, and the chemical processes that take place on far-off stars and planets.

Moon Shots

As we've already seen, our first probes explored the Moon. *Pioneer 4* was the first to take a look as it flew by in 1959. A variety of other unpiloted spacecraft probed, bounced, and photographed. Between 1964 and 1968, NASA had collected thousands of images of the lunar surface. Scientists and engineers needed to know something about the terrain before sending astronauts there. But they also wanted to know more about our nearby neighbor—how it formed, what it was made of, and what its history was.

After completing the Apollo missions in 1972, the United States sent no new missions to the Moon for more than 20 years. *Galileo*, launched in 1989, took a few images on its way to Jupiter, but the next missions designed specifically to study the Moon had to wait until the 1990s.

Clementine, launched in 1994, created extensive maps as it orbited above the Moon's surface. *Lunar Prospector* followed 4 years later. It carried special observational instruments for studying the Moon's surface composition, gas emissions, electromagnetic properties, and gravitational field. *Lunar Prospector* made some startling discoveries. It collected evidence suggesting that the Moon has a tiny core. More importantly, it found that water ice may exist in deep, shadowed crater floors near the Moon's poles.

Ambassadors to the Solar System: The 1970s–1990s

NASA's robot spacecraft also explored the rest of our solar system. In 1962, *Mariner 2* flew by Venus. Since then, NASA spacecraft have visited every planet in the solar system except tiny, distant Pluto. They have flown by, studied, orbited, mapped, and probed. They have scooped up soil, run experiments, and even trundled across the surface in some places. They have visited asteroids, and they have trained their instruments upon the Sun. In the process, NASA's work has greatly transformed our understanding of the neighborhood we live in and its history.

The Sun

At the center of the solar system is the brilliant thermonuclear furnace we call the Sun. Because it is the closest star to Earth, looking closely at how it works gives scientists many keys to understanding the Universe as a whole. Several NASA missions have collected information about the Sun—some of them on their way to do something else. *Pioneers 1, 2, 3,* and *4* were all intended to fly past the Moon on their way to orbit the Sun, but three out of four failed. Four more probes—*Pioneers 6, 7, 8,* and *9*—were launched between 1965 and 1968. They returned extensive information about solar flares.

In the 1970s, the United States and West Germany joined forces and sent two orbiters to study the Sun more closely. The first, *Helios 1,* was launched in 1974. *Helios 2* lifted off in 1976. These spacecraft experienced heat eleven times greater than spacecraft in Earth orbit and provided the first close-up studies of solar dynamics and cosmic rays. During late 1973 and early 1974, astronauts aboard *Skylab* also observed the Sun.

In 1990, the spacecraft *Ulysses* was launched from the Space Shuttle *Discovery.* It was aimed outward toward Jupiter so that it could use the giant planet's mighty gravitational force in a maneuver known as a *gravity assist.* By zooming around Jupiter and swinging back toward the Sun, *Ulysses* was able to move into orbit over the Sun's poles. It approached the Sun's south pole in 1994 and its north pole in 1995.

There, the stalwart spacecraft examined the nature of the Sun's *corona* and magnetic field. It also studied *solar wind*—a plasma, or ionized gas, that originates in the corona and is found throughout the entire solar system.

First Rock

Only one mission has surveyed Mercury. *Mariner 10*, also called *Mariner Venus-Mercury*, was launched in 1973. It flew by Venus for a gravity assist before flying onward. After taking a few pictures of Venus, *Mariner 10* intrigued viewers of Earth with some 12,000 images of the sunlit side of the tiny planet closest to the Sun. Mercury, we learned, looks a lot like the Moon. Its surface is parched and pitted, pockmarked by thousands of craters caused by meteorite impacts. Unlike the Moon, though, Mercury's craters covered almost the entire area photographed by *Mariner 10*.

The innermost planet, Mercury, as viewed by *Mariner 10*

Mariner 10 was the only spacecraft to provide us with close-up views of Mercury.

Mariner 10's reports held another surprise—Mercury has a magnetic field. Usually, a planet produces a magnetic field when it has a rapidly rotating molten iron core. Because Mercury spins nearly sixty times slower than Earth, scientists didn't expect to find any evidence of a magnetic field. Even today, no one can explain the source of Mercury's magnetism.

Earth's Twin

Because Venus is close to Earth and because the two planets are about the same size, some early astronomers thought of Earth and Venus as twin planets. Others believed that Venus might be a garden of Eden—lush, green, warm, and welcoming. The space-age view of Venus proved that both these ideas were wrong.

Venus has been studied by five major NASA missions—*Mariner 2* in 1962, *Mariner 5* in 1967, *Mariner 10* (on its way to Mercury) in 1973, *Pioneer Venus 1* (an orbiter) and *Pioneer Venus 2* (five atmospheric probes) in 1978, and *Magellan* in 1989.

Pioneer Venus 1 used radar to create a detailed map of the surface of Venus. The radar images distinctly showed objects as small as 60 miles (100 km) across and provided scientists with information about 90 percent of the planet's surface. For the first time, humans could peer through Venus's thick, cloudy atmosphere and "see" the surface below. The map showed continent-like highlands, hilly plains, mountains, and flat, barren lowlands.

The surface temperatures on Venus reach a super-scalding 900°F (482°C), making it the hottest planet in the solar system. The *Pioneer Venus 2* probes helped scientists understand why Venus is hotter than Mercury. Equipment on board the spacecraft revealed that the atmosphere of Venus is 96 percent carbon dioxide and nearly 4 percent nitrogen with small amounts of sulfur dioxide, argon, and neon.

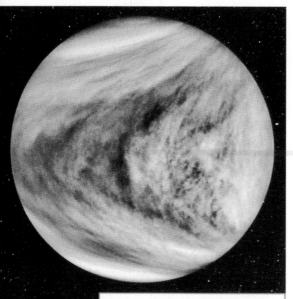

A view of Venus taken by the Pioneer *Venus 1* spacecraft (Background stars have been added to the image.)

Carbon dioxide is a *greenhouse gas*. Like the glass in a greenhouse, the carbon dioxide in a planet's atmosphere allows sunlight to pass through but does not allow heat to escape. Over time, this "greenhouse effect" warms the planet. Because Earth's atmosphere contains a very small amount of carbon dioxide, a greenhouse effect is also at work on our planet.

For the past 150 years, the amount of carbon dioxide in Earth's atmosphere has slowly increased as we burn fossil fuels and large areas of forestland. Are we adding too much carbon dioxide to the atmosphere? Will the greenhouse effect warm Earth too much? Could Earth some day be as hot as Venus is now? Only time will tell.

Magellan, launched in 1989, provided a detailed radar map of almost the entire surface of Venus. This information, combined with data collected by the Mariner missions as well as knowledge gleaned from Soviet missions to Venus, has given scientists a clearer picture of the shrouded planet.

The Red Planet

NASA's Viking missions in 1975 and 1976 sent landers to photograph and test the surface of Mars for signs of life. Although the tests showed no evidence of life on Mars, the question still appears to be open.

Each Viking spacecraft was really two spacecraft in one, an orbiter (on the bottom) and a lander (inside the mushroom-shaped shield on top).

Meanwhile, the Viking orbiters measured the moisture in the Martian atmosphere and took temperature readings of the planet's surface. Photos taken by the Viking orbiters suggest that large quantities of water once flowed over much of Mars's surface.

Mars Pathfinder arrived at the red planet in July 1997. This mission sent a rover named *Sojourner* across the Martian surface to examine rocks and minerals close up—using tools, a camera, and a series of scientific experiments. Researchers on Earth directed the little vehicle by remote control. The mission, which was designed economically and carefully, was a resounding success.

Mars Global Surveyor (MGS) was launched in 1996. It has sent back information that leads scientists to think a great deal of frozen water may still exist below the planet's surface and where there is water, life may have existed at one time. *MGS* carries a high-resolution CCD camera and instruments that allow it to measure magnetic fields, tem-

This is the first color view transmitted to Earth from the surface of Mars. It was taken by the *Viking 1* lander.

perature variations, and the altitudes of surface features. *MGS* is only the first of a series of spacecraft planned for an expanded exploration of Mars in the late 1990s and early twenty-first century.

The Giant Planets

By the 1970s, NASA had begun work on many other exciting missions to the rest of the solar system. These included the long and fruitful journeys made to the outer solar system by *Pioneer 10*, *Pioneer 11*, *Voyager 1*, and *Voyager 2*.

In 1972, NASA launched the first of two Pioneer spacecraft to visit the giants of the outer solar system. *Pioneer 10* flew by Jupiter in 1973. For the first time, we saw close-ups of the big planet's Giant Red Spot—a huge storm system that amateur astronomers can see through their backyard telescopes. Its follow-up companion, *Pioneer 11*, headed for Jupiter in 1973 and arrived there in 1974. Then it continued its journey to the great ringed planet, Saturn. *Pioneer 11* verified that Saturn's rings are composed of chunks of orbiting ice.

The exciting information gained from the *Pioneer* spacecraft was multiplied many times over by the closer, higher-definition images taken by the two Voyager spacecraft that followed. When *Voyager 1* and *Voyager 2* arrived at Jupiter in 1979, they provided close-up views of Jupiter's turbulent, stormy, multicolored clouds. They also sent back images of faint rings around the planet.

Most spectacular, though, were images of the big moons that hover close to Jupiter. Io, Europa, Ganymede, and Callisto are much more fascinating than scientists had imagined. Io is hot and volcanic, spewing sulfur and seething with activity, while Callisto has a lifeless, ancient surface. Europa seems icy and strange, and Ganymede is full of mystery.

This compute-generated composite shows Jupiter and its four largest moons—Callisto, Ganymede, Europa, and Io.

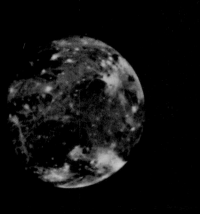

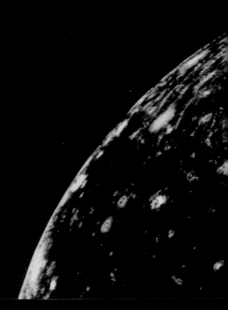

Because scientists were so captivated by these moons, NASA decided to send another spacecraft just to study them. Launched in 1989, *Galileo* returned stunning and intriguing results in 1998 and 1999. One of the biggest surprises was evidence that Europa may have a liquid ocean—and, possibly, some form of life—beneath its icy exterior.

The Voyager visits to Saturn proved equally arresting. The spacecraft sent back more than 70,000 pictures of Saturn and its rings and moons. Scientists received their first close-ups of the turbulence and storms that rage in Saturn's cloud-tops. Stunning views of the rings destroyed theories about a simple, ordered structure. Voyager images revealed immense complexity and a constantly changing system made up of tens of thousands of interacting ringlets. The spacecraft also discovered that "shepherd moons" in the rings seem to help keep order.

Views of Saturn's icy moon, Titan, and its hazy, orange atmosphere intrigued scientists so much that NASA launched the *Cassini-Huygens* spacecraft in September 1997 to take a closer look at both Saturn and Titan. When the mission arrives, the Huygens probe will break away and descend to the surface of the big moon, while Cassini orbiter continues to collect data from above.

Voyager 2 traveled on to Uranus and Neptune. Images of Uranus revealed the planet's smooth, blue-green cloud tops and thin rings of Uranus with shepherd moons much like the ones orbiting Saturn. The spacecraft also revealed ten previously unidentified moons and provided images close-up of the "big five"—Miranda, Ariel, Umbriel, Titania, and Oberon. Scientists were intrigued by Miranda's tortured surface.

Voyager 2 took another 3 years to reach Neptune, arriving in 1989. On Earth, NASA linked together every large antenna possible to receive the faint and distant signals. Images from the probe showed a

An artist's interpretation of the Huygens probe breaking away from the Cassini orbiter as they near Saturn

bluish planet with a swirling, stormy cloud structure and rings in the form of segmented arcs with thin connections that completed the circles. The big surprise came, though, from Neptune's biggest moon, Triton. It seemed to have huge, spouting geysers or plumes of dark material erupting from its surface.

Looking at Asteroids

Often called the "leftovers of the solar system," asteroids have received a lot of attention in recent years. We know that someday, one of these space boulders could head toward Earth on a crash course. A dedicated group of astronomers thinks that finding out more about asteroids is vital to our planet's continued well-being. As a result, NASA has spent more time studying them in the last decade. *Galileo*, launched in 1989, gave us our first asteroid close-up as it flew by Gaspra and Ida on its way to Jupiter. The *NEAR* (Near Earth Asteroid Rendezvous) spacecraft, launched in 1996, was designed to visit and orbit the asteroid Eros.

Next Stop: The Universe

Beyond our solar system, the Universe beckons—with its galaxies and stars, its newly found solar systems, and its vast expanses. Scientists have explored astrophysical questions whenever they could by including experiments on NASA's spacecraft, but some of the most spectacular discoveries about the Universe have come from NASA's space-based observatories.

One of the earliest was the *Infrared Astronomical Satellite,* which operated for a year in 1983. It returned images and data that provided an important base for astronomers to work from. Most importantly, the satellite identified dust and gas rings around many stars.

In the early 1990s, the *Cosmic Background Explorer* (*COBE*) stunned the world by looking out—almost to the beginning of time— with an instrument known as a far infrared absolute spectrophotome- ter. Data collected by *COBE* ended a debate that had been raging among astrophysicists and astronomers for decades: How did the Uni- verse begin? *COBE* provided solid evidence of the Big Bang theory— the idea that the Universe originated with a violent explosion.

In 1989, astronomers welcomed NASA's launch of the *Hubble Space Telescope* (*HST*), named after American astronomer Edwin P. Hubble. Long awaited, this space-based astronomical observatory had the potential to show scientists distant objects as they truly appear. (Earth's thick atmosphere distorts our view of objects in space.)

Unfortunately, the first images returned from the *HST* were not as clear as expected. The telescope's main mirror had a flaw. After the *HST* was repaired in 1993, though, it began to transform our ideas and resolve some of our questions about the Universe. *HST* could look back 11 billion years—all the way to the dawn of the Universe. It revealed new layers of galaxies—some 40 billion of them—so distant that they are practically invisible to viewers on Earth. It also captured images of the broken pieces of Comet Shoemaker-Levy 9 as they exploded against the cloud-tops of Jupiter in 1993 and has taken the

In December 1993, spacewalking Space Shuttle astronauts teamed up to correct the vision of the ailing *Hubble Space Telescope*. Thomas Akers is inside the telescope bay, assisting Kathryn Thornton (just visible at the end of the giant arm of the Shuttle's Remote Manipulator System) as she installs a 640-pound (290-kg) corrective instrument.

best photos we have of Pluto. Each day, NASA posts stunning images on the Internet of far-off galaxies, *novas*, double stars, and red giants. Thousands of people all over the world can view these photos on their computers and marvel at the complexity and beauty of the Universe.

By 1996, twenty-three space-based telescopes were in operation. One of these was *Ulysses*, the mission to the Sun mentioned earlier. Another, the *Chandra X-ray Observatory*, was launched in 1999. It has

Chandra: A Luminous Mind

NASA's most advanced X-ray observatory, the *Chandra X-ray Observatory*, was launched from the Space Shuttle in July 1999. It was named after the great Indian-American astrophysicist Subrahmanyan Chandrasekhar. Everyone called him Chandra, which means "luminous" or "Moon" in an ancient Indian language called Sanskrit.

Chandra was a kind, gentle man and a brilliant thinker. Physicist Hans Bethe, who won a Nobel prize in 1967, once described Chandra as "a first-rate astrophysicist and a beautiful and warm human being."

In 1937, Chandra came to the United States with his wife, Lalitha, to teach at the University of Chicago. He contributed to our understanding of the Universe in at least seven major areas, from white dwarf stars to black holes. Chandra is considered one of the greatest astrophysicists of the twentieth century. In 1983, he received the Nobel Prize in physics for his work in theoretical physics related to the structure and evolution of the stars. He once described his work as a "quest after perspectives."

In the words of Martin Rees, Great Britain's Astronomer Royal, "Chandra probably thought longer and deeper about our Universe than anyone since Einstein." Subrahmanyan Chandrasekhar died in August 1995, but his tradition of intense inquiry lives on in the *Chandra X-ray Observatory*, which searches the Universe for new insights into its structure and history.

The *Chandra X-ray Observatory* is named for Subrahmanyan "Chandra" Chandrasekhar, an Indian-American Nobel-prize-winning astrophysicist.

sent us exciting images of explosive galaxies, remnants of supernovas, and more. It promises to change our understanding greatly as it continues to focus its X-ray imager on exploding stars, collapsing stars, expanding clouds of superhot gas, and black holes.

NASA's commitment to the quest for knowledge is nowhere more evident than in its range of programs for planetary exploration and the study of the Universe—and its research into the secrets of that important planet known as Earth.

Chapter 6

Mission to Planet Earth

Not all NASA's inquiries into the nature of the solar system are directed at other planets. From the time we first saw Earthrise from the Moon, we have developed a new view of our planet. Our explorations of other planets have shown us how unique our own planet is, and we have come to recognize its fragility.

At Mars and Venus, we have seen processes that also take place here on Earth. As a result, we now understand that our atmosphere, like the atmosphere of Venus, could one day experience an extreme greenhouse effect. It is also possible that our planet could become an airless desert like Mars. Earth is tiny and vulnerable in the vast Universe—a sort of spaceship on which we travel. It requires our constant and attentive care.

Since the late 1950s, when *Sputnik* and *Explorer* first circled the globe, thousands of satellites have entered Earth orbit. They are our eyes and ears in space. They keep tabs on how our planet is doing. They provide detailed maps of the oceans and landmasses. They also report on the state of the atmosphere. These space-based laboratories have even helped scientists understand our planet's history and geological formation.

Imaging satellites also act as spies. Military powers can use them to pinpoint troop movements and spot arms factories. The United States has used reconnaissance satellites to observe troop movements in troubled areas of Eastern Europe and to spot terrorist hideouts. The world has become a much more public place, where evil intentions have become harder to hide. Legitimate defense plans have also become much more difficult to keep safely secret.

Communications satellites beam signals to Earth from orbit. The results are usually amazingly clear and reliable. The history of these satellites goes all the way back to December 1958, when the United States launched an Atlas rocket into orbit to beam a taped message from President Eisenhower to radio listeners.

The Signal Communication by Orbiting Relay Equipment (SCORE) satellite, launched in 1960, relayed radio waves bounced up from Earth. The 52-inch (132-cm) sphere could pass teletype, voice, and fax data from its origin on Earth back down to another location. Also in 1960, NASA launched *Echo 1*, a 100-foot (30-m) aluminum-coated balloon that acted as a relay satellite. It allowed the first two-way communication via satellite. Bell Labs used *Echo 1* to send the first transoceanic satellite message to Paris a few days after the satellite began orbiting Earth.

This technology rapidly attracted the communications industry. AT&T (the American Telephone and Telegraph Company) soon joined Bell Labs in developing the first commercial satellite. *Telstar 1* was launched in 1962. Composed of solar cells and an antenna, *Telstar* transmitted the first live television signal across the Atlantic on its first day of operation. The transmission left the United States, traveled to England and France, and then

In 1989, scientists and engineers at NASA announced an ambitious program called the U.S. Global Change Research Program. The goal of the program was to keep tabs on all Earth's vital signs. The original idea involved a fleet of satellites that would monitor changes in our planet's *biosphere*. That includes the entire Earth, with all the

back again. The enterprise fueled imaginations worldwide and was soon followed by many more communications satellites with names such as Syncom, Intelsat, "Early Bird," and Comsat.

Today, industry, small businesses, and individuals alike rely on information supplied by satellites. Examples include mobile voice communication via satellite, knowledge bases on the Internet, satellite-relayed television programs, remote sensing images from space, and location data from the Global Positioning System satellites.

Mobile telephone communication can now bypass the bottleneck of telephone lines and reach rural and remote areas not served by conventional telephones. By the 1990s, people in Iran began to place $700 satellite dishes on their rooftops to watch World Cup soccer matches or the British Broadcasting Company instead of Iranian state-controlled broadcasting.

Everyone can benefit from the Global Positioning System (GPS), a satellite system originally developed by the U.S. military to pinpoint a Navy vessel's position at

This team of spacewalking astronauts—Richard Hieb, Thomas Akers, and Pierre Thuot—captured an Intelsat satellite in May 1992.

sea. Motorists looking for the best route can now get a GPS readout, scientists can track members of a wolf pack, and emergency crews can locate a victim who dialed 911.

Satellites have become a way of life.

organisms that live here and everything that makes life here possible. Eventually, the name of the program was changed to Mission to Planet Earth. In recent years, budget cuts have forced scientists and researchers at NASA to restructure their original plan, but NASA officials remain committed to the program.

Watching the Weather

Before the space age, weather prediction was largely guesswork based on limited local instruments. Today, we routinely see color satellite images on our television screens, and we can easily call up weather data and images for any part of the world on the Internet.

NASA launched its first meteorological satellite—*TIROS 1* (Television and Infrared Observation Satellite)—in 1960. Between 1960 and 1965, *TIROS* satellites aimed television cameras at Earth and sent back more than 500,000 pictures of worldwide weather systems. More sophisticated Nimbus satellites followed.

Weather satellites proved to be a powerful new tool for meteorologists. They provided images of hurricanes forming and moving toward landmasses. They also allowed us to see how warm and cold air masses interact.

In 1973, the *Nimbus 7* weather satellite began keeping track of a portion of our atmosphere called the ozone layer. Produced through the interaction of solar energy and oxygen, ozone (O_3) protects all living things from the Sun's damaging ultraviolet (UV) rays. In the mid-1980s, scientists noticed that a hole in the ozone layer recurred each year between September and October. What's more, each year it grew a little bigger.

Scientists soon realized that ozone was being destroyed by chlorofluorocarbons (CFCs)—chemicals used as coolants in air-conditioning systems and refrigerators and to power aerosol spray cans. Many countries have now banned the use of CFCs. Hopefully, the ozone layer will be able to rebuild itself. If so, it will be thanks to the early warning provided by a little satellite named Nimbus. Additional reports continue to come in from NASA's Total Ozone Mapping Spectrometer (TOMS)

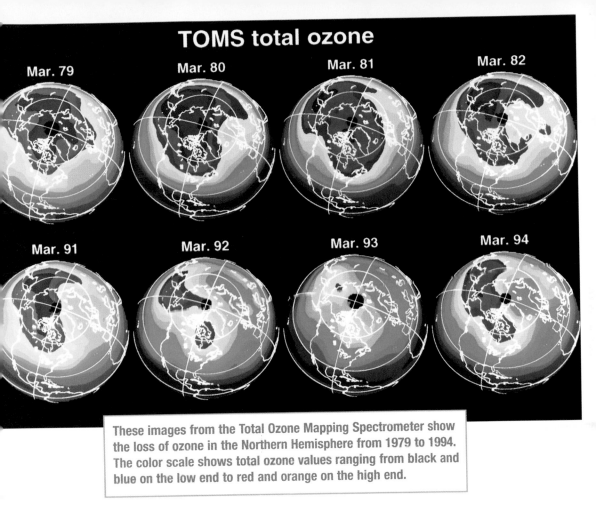

TOMS total ozone

Mar. 79   Mar. 80   Mar. 81   Mar. 82

Mar. 91   Mar. 92   Mar. 93   Mar. 94

These images from the Total Ozone Mapping Spectrometer show the loss of ozone in the Northern Hemisphere from 1979 to 1994. The color scale shows total ozone values ranging from black and blue on the low end to red and orange on the high end.

to help monitor ozone levels.

In the late 1990s, a joint effort between the United States and France known as *TOPEX/Poseidon* delivered images that have given scientists clues about El Niño—a phenomenon that periodically causes extensive flooding and extreme weather patterns. *TOPEX/Poseidon* shows the changes in ocean-wave height and average sea level that accompany El Niño. The satellite's reports are currently helping scientists predict El Niño events at least a year in advance. This allows people to prepare for the harsh weather associated with El Niño.

In 2003, NASA's Jet Propulsion Laboratory plans to launch a new observatory called *CloudSat*. This satellite will use advanced radar to

Technicians performing a preflight check of *Landsat 4* before its 1982 launch

look at the vertical structure of clouds. (Current weather satellites can only catch images of the topmost layer of clouds.) *CloudSat* will also be the first satellite to study clouds worldwide, and it will look especially at the transfer of solar energy to and from Earth's atmosphere. The information should help us understand climate changes on global, regional, and even local scales.

The Lay of the Land

In July 1972, the first *Earth Resources Technology Satellite (ERTS)* was launched into Earth orbit. This series of satellites, which later received the more widely known name, "Landsat," has had a long life. In fact, Landsat satellites are still sending us stunning views of Earth.

Scientists have used Landsat images to monitor environmental changes, pollution, and land-use management. The satellites have also helped civil engineers plan large projects, such as dams. They have provided information about ice floes and the location of natural resources, and have even spotted archaeological remains that no one knew about. In April 1986, when a nuclear reactor exploded in Chernobyl, Ukraine, a Landsat satellite passed overhead shortly afterward. Within 72 hours, a digital image of radioactivity pouring out of the reactor had been broadcast all over the world.

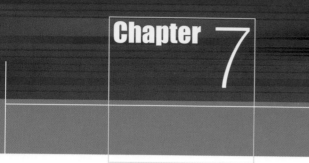

Chapter 7

Living and Working in Space

For nearly 40 years, NASA astronauts have worked high above Earth's surface. From the beginning of the space program, being an astronaut has meant working in space—not just piloting spacecraft. Astronauts and other specialists routinely try out new hardware. They also test the effects of zero gravity or microgravity on people and other living things as well as on substances. Astronauts have also launched satellites, made important repairs, and built structures in space. Since the 1980s, they have done most of their work aboard one of NASA's Space Shuttle missions.

Commuting to Work in Space

The Space Shuttle has proven to be both one of the most successful—as well as one of the most controversial—NASA programs. Each shuttle consists of a reusable orbiter with a two-level control cabin and solid fuel boosters plus a giant external liquid-fuel tank that is discarded during flight. The orbiter has three main engines, each capable of producing 375,000 pounds (170,000 kg) of thrust. Smaller auxiliary engines give the orbiter its final push into orbit. The orbiter has wings and landing wheels, so it can land on a runway like an airplane.

Originally, NASA had hoped to create a fully reusable space vehicle, but budget cuts made it impossible to design and build such a

The Space Shuttle *Columbia* launching from Kennedy Space Center in Florida on July 1, 1997

spacecraft. What NASA ended up with was a compromise. Although it is not completely reusable, the shuttle is more economical and efficient than previous space vehicles.

The first shuttle tests took place on February 18, 1977. Later that year and the next, astronauts tested the *Enterprise* orbiter within Earth's atmosphere. The debut in space for the Space Transportation System (the shuttle system's official name) took place on April 21, 1981. As the orbiter *Columbia* (STS-1) stood on the launchpad, its glistening white body looked like an enormous airplane standing on end. It rode piggyback atop a huge liquid-fuel engine flanked by two solid-fuel rockets.

After several delays, the countdown began. More than 2,000 reporters and 300,000 spectators watched with anticipation as the engines roared and *Columbia* climbed skyward. Moments later, the rocket engines fell away. Less than 10 minutes after takeoff, the huge, white bird ascended into orbit 170 miles (274 km) above Earth.

Two days later, *Columbia* returned to Earth, landing at Edwards Air Force Base in California. The mission had been a tremendous success. The first flight of the *Columbia* (STS-1) was followed by three more test flights. The astronauts on STS-3 tested the remote manipulator arm, which has since become an invaluable tool. The first fully operational flight of the shuttle was STS-5. The orbiter carried scientific experiments and launched a satellite. In addition, an EVA was performed inside the payload bay by astronauts Story Musgrave and Donald Peterson. The seventh shuttle flight, which launched in June 1983, carried Sally K. Ride into orbit. She was the first female American astronaut.

The Space Shuttle *Columbia* touching down at Edwards Air Force Base in California

Despite these successes, some people remained critical of the Space Shuttle program. Some experts thought the money would be better spent on planetary and scientific research done by robot spacecraft. Others thought NASA should develop a more straightforward design that could both take off and land like an airplane. In other words, it should have remained true to its original purpose—a "shuttle" or taxi between Earth and a space station. Instead, the shuttle became a satellite launcher and a space lab.

Critics continue to argue that satellites can be launched more economically by other means. They also claim that a space laboratory belongs on a space station, where continuing experiments can take place. Of course, building a space station is a big job, and construction was slow to begin. So the space shuttle has filled in, serving many more purposes than originally planned.

"Routine" Becomes Catastrophe

Soon the Space Shuttle fleet included three new shuttles—*Atlantis, Discovery,* and *Challenger.* The Space Shuttle proved so successful that its launches and landings became almost as routine as the scheduled flights of a regular airline. Spaceflight had become an ordinary, everyday experience rather than an exciting event. It was so safe, so predictable, and so repetitive that it no longer excited or interested the general public.

That attitude suddenly changed on January 28, 1986. Just 73 seconds after the Space Shuttle *Challenger* lifted off, smoke began shooting out from the cluster of giant rocket engines that thrust it into the sky. An enormous explosion followed, and *Challenger* broke into pieces and fell to the ocean. The orbiter was lost and every member of the seven-person crew died. Lost were Francis R. (Dick) Scobee, Michael J. Smith, Judith A. Resnik, Ronald E. McNair, Ellison S. Onizuka, Gregory B. Jarvis, and Christa McAuliffe. McAuliffe was a young elementary-school teacher who had been chosen to become the first "teacher in space," and thousands of schoolchildren were watching the launch on classroom television sets. Around the world, billions of people witnessed the accident on television and mourned the *Challenger* crew.

An intense investigation followed to discover the reasons for the accident. As a result, no Space Shuttle missions were launched for

On January 28, 1986, Americans were startled when *Challenger* exploded a few seconds after takeoff.

more than a year and a half. During that period, only the brilliant photos and details returned to us from the *Voyager 2* spacecraft as it flew by the faraway planet Uranus reminded Americans that they knew how to make things work in space.

Science at Work: The O-Ring that Froze

The day of the *Challenger* accident was cold and icy. Icicles hung from the shuttle. Pictures taken shortly after the rockets fired show a small puff of black smoke coming from the lower end of the right rocket booster. This was a spot where o-shaped rings, known as "O-rings," were used to seal a joint.

The investigators finally concluded that the cold weather at Kennedy Space Center that day had made the rings so brittle that they no longer held their seal. Right after liftoff, the smoke seemed to disappear—probably because heat from the engine softened the O-rings enough to reseal the joint. But the wind was brisk and *Challenger* was sharply buffeted as it rose skyward.

Normally, the shuttle would have taken the beating well, but the damaged O-rings apparently couldn't take it, and they broke again. This time the rupture did not reseal, and a flame burst from the joint. The rest is tragic history.

Further investigation revealed that several workers had expressed concern about the O-rings. But because production crews were under a great deal of pressure, they had not paid enough attention to the situation. Good management, clear communication, and heightened concern for quality had to be emphasized if NASA wanted the shuttle to be safe again. To address these concerns, NASA created a new Office of Safety, Reliability, Maintainability, and Quality Assurance.

On September 29, 1988, NASA launched STS-26 *Discovery*. The flight was a complete success. The 1990s brought many more successful shuttle flights. Many of these missions launched satellites. In 1990, the *Hubble Space Telescope* was placed in orbit from the shuttle. When it proved to have a flawed mirror, NASA *Endeavour* astronauts became heroes in 1993 by performing an EVA repair mission to install a set of corrective lenses. More than two dozen scientific missions have also flown since 1988. Many of these involved *Spacelab*—a reusable laboratory designed by the European Space Agency to fit in the bay of the shuttle.

Astronauts on *Mir*

While NASA was building space shuttles, the USSR developed its piloted space program in another direction. The Soviets were interested in the human endurance challenges posed by long-term missions in space. Beginning in the 1970s, they built a series of space stations that astronauts could live on for long periods of time. Shuttle craft could be launched with supplies and trade-off crews, but usually one member of the crew remained aboard for an extended period of time—often as long as a year.

The last of the Soviet space stations to be launched was *Mir* (meaning "Peace"), which welcomed its first crew in February 1986—a month after the United States lost *Challenger*. For more than a decade, *Mir* housed scientific experiments and long-term, three-person crews.

These three *Mir* crew members began their work aboard the space station in 1995. In this photo, they are shown aboard the U.S. Space Shuttle *Atlantis*'s Docking Module, which transported them to *Mir*.

During the 1990s, several U.S. astronauts joined Russian cosmonauts on board *Mir*. Between February 21 and September 1, 1996, Shannon Lucid, a 55-year-old veteran U.S. astronaut, spent 188 days on *Mir* with Russian cosmonauts Yuri Onufrienko and Yuri Usachev.

Shannon Lucid: Ambassador to *Mir*

Shannon Lucid—a biochemist, pilot, and mother of three children—approached her adventure aboard the Russian space station *Mir* with a sense of humor and good spirits.

Because *Mir* orbited Earth so rapidly, the Sun "rose" every 45 minutes, and Lucid found that she had trouble keeping track of time. To help solve this problem, she established a Sunday tradition of wearing pink socks and sharing a bag of Jello with the Russian cosmonauts.

The crew aboard *Mir* received supplies from an autopiloted Russian spacecraft called *Progress*. In her journal, Lucid wrote what it was like to watch *Progress* approach: "To me, it looked like some alien insect headed straight toward us. All of a sudden I really did feel like I was in a 'cosmic outpost' anxiously awaiting supplies—and really hoping that my family remembered to send me some books and candy!"

Lucid performed many scientific experiments while she was aboard the Russian space station, including several for the Canadian Space Agency. By the end of her mission, she had traveled 75.2 million miles (121 million km).

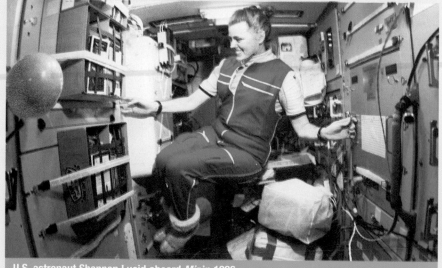

U.S. astronaut Shannon Lucid aboard *Mir* in 1996

By the end of her stay, she had logged more flight hours in orbit than any other woman in the world and the most flight hours in orbit by any non-Russian.

A New Space Habitat

Some of the Space Shuttles launched in the 1990s tested equipment and construction techniques that scientists and engineers developed for achieving an incredible goal—the construction of an *International Space Station.*

Although NASA officials knew they could develop the technology to make this incredible dream come true, at first they lacked the funding to get the project off the ground. They had trouble getting Congress to provide financial support for the project.

Some people worried that other nations who said they would help build the station might back out. If that happened, the U.S. expenditures would be money lost. Of course, every time this issue was debated in Congress, other countries already contributing to the project worried that they would be left in the lurch. Finally, though, in 1998, the first piece of the *International Space Station* was placed in orbit by a Russian rocket. Additional pieces were added by Space Shuttle crews. As many as sixteen nations have contributed to the project.

The first parts were assembled, and a new permanent human presence in space soon began to seem realistic. None too soon, either. The orbit of *Mir* was beginning to deteriorate, and the big Soviet space station was starting to show its age. Scientists hope that the *International Space Station* can replace *Mir* as a permanent habitat in space where scientific work and manufacturing can take place. And, eventually, they hope that it can serve as a depot, or way station, for distant voyages to the edges of our solar system and beyond.

Space Spin-offs

NASA has always been committed to passing useful devices, techniques, and technologies on to the public, so that everyone benefits from the space program's research and development (R&D). The number of useful "spin-offs" from the space program is now in the thousands.

Our lives have literally been transformed by space-age technology. We watch TV programs beamed in by satellite. We fasten our jackets with Velcro fasteners developed to help astronauts work in zero-gravity. We use miniaturized computer chips in our microwave ovens. The list goes on and on.

Recently, NASA has begun forming R&D partnerships with small businesses, research laboratories, and universities to develop products for both NASA and the public at the same time. You'd be surprised how many ways these partnerships can touch your life.

- At an on-the-job training seminar, you might use a self-paced multimedia training program based on the interactive training techniques and software used by astronauts.
- To improve airline safety, many pilots are now trained with easy-to-use 3-D simulation software based on NASA simulators.
- The catalytic converter in your the family's car may have been derived from an ultra-compact catalytic converter developed for spacecraft life support.
- What about the pacemaker that regulates your grandfather's heartbeat? Thanks to technologies developed by NASA, some pacemakers now have rechargeable, long-life batteries. They use a single chip derived from micro-miniaturization technology developed to fit complex equipment on small spacecraft. The same communication system that allows NASA engineers to reprogram satellites allows a physician reprogram a pacemaker inside the patient's body without surgery.

- Wind tunnels at NASA's Langley Research Center helped Cessna develop an efficient high-speed business-class jet that races across the sky at 51,000 feet (15,544 m) and a speed of Mach 0.92—nearly the speed of sound.
- What do porpoises and NASA payload retrievers have in common? New England fisheries often catch harbor porpoises by mistake in their nets. The porpoises become entangled and die when they can't surface to breathe. Believe it or not, NASA engineers have developed something that could help save the animals.

When a payload from space splashes down in icy ocean waters, NASA needs a way to locate it for retrieval. Engineers developed a device that can withstand a forceful impact and emit a signal in all directions for many hours. A private company used that technology to develop a low-cost device that emits a signal warning porpoises to stay away from fishing nets.

Chapter 8

NASA in the Twenty-First Century

The twenty-first century promises a bright future for NASA. It will be filled with new advances, challenges, and opportunities. Soon there may be settlements on the Moon and Mars. Asteroid miners may ship precious cargo back to Earth. Space tourists may one day zip around the solar system, snapping pictures of the *International Space Station* and other space attractions.

Scientists may even discover some kind of life form on Jupiter's moon, Europa, or detect signals sent from an advanced civilization that lives on a planet in a nearby solar system. Scientists may finally figure out how the Universe began as well as how and where life began.

In this artist's conception of the *International Space Station*, the black rectangles represent the solar panels that will provide the space station all its power.

They may even come to understand how galaxies, stars, and planetary systems form and evolve.

Faster, better, and cheaper are the keywords for NASA as it moves into the twenty-first century, but its vision still remains large. NASA is currently working on plans for continued exploration of the solar system, including more visits to Mars and the icy surface of Jupiter's moon, Europa. In addition, a new generation of space telescopes will seek out planets around distant stars and will try to find answers to the many questions scientists still have about galaxies, stars, and the evolution of solar systems.

The early years of the twenty-first century will see a steady stream of small robot-spacecraft swooping around the solar system to study the Sun, neighboring planets, comets, and asteroids.

In 1998, the spacecraft *Deep Space 1* set off to visit asteroid 1992KD and a comet. It will travel part of the way under ion engine power. Although the mission will provide more information about asteroids, its primary goal is to test the use of ion engines for travel in deep space.

Standard rocket engines burn chemical fuels to propel spacecraft, but an ion engine uses electrically charged xenon gas—an element similar to neon. The electrical power comes from solar panels on the spacecraft. The electricity charges the xenon gas, setting up a reaction that causes the charged gas to shoot very fast out of the engine as exhaust. The principle of action and reaction is the same as for chemical-burning rockets, but ion engines use fuel ten times more efficiently. And although their initial thrust is ten times less forceful, ion engines can achieve great speeds over time. As a result, spacecraft using ion engines can actually arrive at their destinations sooner than spacecraft powered by conventional engines.

Humans in Space

For the time being, human activity in space will most likely remain focused on activities in Earth orbit aboard the Space Shuttle and the *International Space Station.* Eventually, though, NASA will develop new space vehicles. The Space Shuttle has certainly proved its value, but it is an expensive and imperfect vehicle for transporting cargo and passengers from Earth to orbit.

NASA and many private space companies are working on designs for vehicles to replace the shuttle. Some of these vehicles are already in the testing stages. Two experimental "space planes," the X-33 and the X-34, are among the front-runners. These two programs are part of a larger program known as the Reusable Launch Vehicle (RLV) Technology Program, a cooperative venture among NASA, the U.S. Air Force, and private industry. The overall goal of the RLV program is to

An artist's representation of the X-33 experimental space plane

develop simple, reusable Earth-to-orbit spacecraft that NASA could operate in much the same ways as conventional airliners.

The self-contained, single-stage vehicle would take off and land much like an airplane, and, like an airplane, it would also be completely reusable. Such a vehicle would eliminate the need for the complicated, expensive rocket boosters we see today. Imagine the Space Shuttle taking off from a runway, instead of being attached to big rocket boosters. That picture gives you a rough idea of what an RLV might look like. Scaled-down models of the X-33 and X-34 have already begun testing some of the principles of RLV technology.

NASA is also looking at some even more experimental Earth-to-orbit systems, such as the Magnetic Levitation Launcher. Some high-speed trains in Japan already use magnetic levitation for propulsion. This system relies on high-strength magnets to lift and propel objects forward on a cushion of air above a track.

To launch objects from Earth to orbit, NASA envisions something similar to a flatbed railroad car carrying the object to be launched. Using magnetic levitation, the car would travel above a long track at 600 miles (965 km) per hour. At the track's end, the car would catapult skyward. Then, as the carrier becomes airborne, the system would switch to a rocket engine for the power to reach orbit. The Magnetic Levitation Launcher is just in the "we're looking into it" stage, but it is a good example of NASA's search for faster and cheaper Earth-to-orbit systems.

As the twenty-first century progresses, scientists should begin to understand much more about the potential and limitations of human beings in space. NASA's longer-range plans hint at a crewed mission—a settlement on the Moon, or even, perhaps, the long-dreamed-of human expedition to Mars.

For many people, both inside and outside NASA, the dream of putting human beings on Mars has become the natural sequel to NASA's Moon expeditions. Technologically, the voyage to Mars would be difficult. Such a journey would require major advances in space-propulsion systems as well as communication and life-support systems. But such a mission would represent a major breakthrough in the human exploration and settlement of space. It would make the twenty-first century truly the "Age of Space." It would open the doors to all the wonders and dreams of the early space pioneers.

Into the Future

By the end of the twenty-first century, we will certainly have a better understanding of the nature and history of our solar system. We will also have discovered much more about both the fragility and the resilience of our own planet Earth.

An artist's view of exobiologists and geologists exploring Mars

NASA's history offers a rich legacy of big visions. That tradition will continue far into the future. Although our dreams may sometimes be greater than available financial resources or technology, scientists and engineers will continue to work toward these goals. The history of NASA has shown us that when enough people support an idea, they will find a way to make their vision a reality.

Humans will continue to be interested in the mysteries of space, and NASA will continue to develop the technology that allows us to explore the vast expanses beyond Earth's atmosphere. Despite its shaky political beginnings and its current fight for funding, the heart of NASA will continue to beat with the same far-reaching dreams that have already taken people to the Moon and robotic spacecraft to the edges of our solar system. As the Russian space visionary Konstantin Tsiolkovsky (1857–1935) once wrote, "The Earth is the cradle of the mind, but we cannot live forever in a cradle."

1957 — USSR puts the first artificial satellite, *Sputnik 1*, into Earth-orbit.

USSR launches *Sputnik 2* into Earth-orbit.

1958 — The United States successfully launches an artificial satellite, *Explorer 1*, into Earth-orbit.

The second U.S. satellite, *Vanguard 1*, achieves Earth-orbit.

NASA begins operations.

1959 — *Pioneer 4* flies by the Moon.

The USSR's *Luna 2* lands on the Moon.

1960 — The United States launches the first successful weather satellite, *TIROS 1*. NASA launches Echo 1, first communications satellite.

1961 — NASA launches *Freedom 7*, the first piloted Mercury spacecraft.

President John F. Kennedy proposes that NASA should land a man on the Moon by the end of the decade.

NASA launches the second piloted Mercury space-craft, *Liberty Bell 7*.

Ranger 1 is launched to survey and map the Moon, but it fails to achieve orbit.

The Manned Spacecraft Center is founded in Houston, Texas. It was renamed the Lyndon B. Johnson Space Center in 1973.

The Mississippi Test Facility is founded. It was renamed the John C. Stennis Space Center in 1988.

1962 — John Glenn orbits Earth in the *Friendship 7* Mercury spacecraft.

Ranger 4 becomes the first U.S. spacecraft to land on the Moon.

Telstar 1, the first privately built satellite, is launched.

Mariner 2 completes a flyby of Venus.

1963 — NASA launches *Faith 7*, the final Mercury mission.

1964 — *Ranger 6* lands on the Moon, but its cameras fail.

First unpiloted test flight of a Gemini spacecraft.

First unpiloted test flight of the Apollo Command Module in orbit.

Ranger 7 lunar impact probe reaches the Moon.

Mariner 4 makes the first successful Mars flyby.

1965 — *Ranger 8* and *Ranger 9* make lunar impact tests.

Gus Grissom and John Young make the first piloted flight of the Gemini program in *Gemini 3*.

The first American EVA takes place during *Gemini 4* mission.

Gemini 5 is launched.

Gemini 6-A, piloted by astronauts Wally Schirra and Tom Stafford, completes a rendezvous with *Gemini 7*, piloted by astronauts Frank Borman and Jim Lovell, who set a record for time spent in space.

1966 — First docking of one spacecraft with another is accomplished by astronauts Neil Armstrong and David Scott during the *Gemini 8* mission.

The USSR achieves lunar orbit on April 6 with its *Luna 10* unpiloted space probe.

NASA's unpiloted *Surveyor 1* makes a successful soft landing on the Moon and sends back thousands of photographs.

Astronauts Tom Stafford and Eugene Cernan fly *Gemini 9-A.*

Aboard Gemini 10, astronauts Mike Collins and John Young complete two rendezvous, docking maneuvers, and a complicated EVA.

Lunar Orbiter 1 successfully orbits the Moon. *Lunar Orbiter 2* follows a few months later.

Astronauts Pete Conrad and Richard Gordon make the *Gemini 11* flight.

During the last Gemini flight, *Gemini 12*, Jim Lovell and Buzz Aldrin, complete three EVAs.

1967 — During a test of the *Apollo 1* command module, astronauts Gus Grissom, Ed White, and Roger Chaffee die of asphyxiation caused by a flash fire. The Apollo program is put on hold while the space craft is redesigned for greater safety.

NASA launches *Lunar Orbiter 3* and *Lunar Orbiter 4*. *Surveyor 3* makes a successful lunar landing.

Mariner 5 makes a successful Venus flyby

NASA launches the *Explorer 35* IMP-E lunar orbiter and *Lunar Orbiter 5*. *Surveyor 5* and *Surveyor 6* make successful lunar landings.

The X-15 experimental rocket plane piloted by Major William J. Knight travels 4,534 miles (7,297 km) per hour (mach 6.72) and sets a speed record.

1968 — *Surveyor 7* makes a successful lunar landing.

The USSR launches the *Luna 14* lunar orbiter.

The unpiloted Soviet spacecraft *Zond 5* and *Zond 6* fly around the Moon and return to Earth—an important first.

In the first piloted flight of the Apollo spacecraft in Earth orbit, astronauts Wally Schirra, Donn F. Eisele, and Walter Cunningham fly Apollo 7.

Apollo 8 becomes the first crewed spacecraft to orbit the Moon.

1969

Mariner 6 and *Mariner 7* complete successful Mars flybys.

James McDivitt, David Scott, and Russell Schweickart orbit Earth in *Apollo 9* and run a test of all the hardware, including the lunar module.

Apollo 10 astronauts Eugene Cernan, John Young, and Tom Stafford run the last dress rehearsal for the landing on the Moon.

During the *Apollo 11* mission, Mike Collins pilots the command module while astronauts Neil Armstrong and Buzz Aldrin become the first humans to walk on the Moon.

The USSR's *Zond 7* makes a lunar flyby and returns to Earth.

Apollo 12 completes its mission.

1970 — The *Apollo 13* crew—Jim Lowell, Fred Haise, and John Swigert—are forced to return to Earth due an explosion in the service module of their spacecraft.

The USSR sends a lander named *Venera 7* to Venus.

The USSR's *Luna 16* collects a sample of lunar material and returns to Earth.

The unpiloted *Zond 8* completes a lunar flyby and returns to Earth.

The USSR launches *Luna 17/Lunokhod 1* unpiloted lunar rover mission.

1971 — *Apollo 14* completes a successful lunar landing.

NASA attempts a Mars flyby with *Mariner 8*, but suffers a launch failure.

The USSR sends *Mars 2* and *Mars 3*, two orbiter/landers, to Mars. The orbiters are successful, but the landers fail.

Mariner 9 orbits Mars.

Apollo 15 completes a successful lunar landing.

The USSR sends *Luna 19* to Moon.

1972 — The *Luna 20* unpiloted mission collects a lunar sample and returns to Earth.

Pioneer 10 sets out to fly by Jupiter.

The USSR sends *Venera 8* to Venus.

Apollo 16 and *Apollo 17* complete successful lunar landings.

1973 — USSR's *Luna 21/Lunokhod 2* completes an unpiloted lunar rover mission.

Pioneer 11 sets out to fly by Jupiter and Saturn.

NASA launches *Explorer 49* RAE-B, a lunar orbiter/radio astronomy lab.

The USSR launches a series of Mars missions. Only *Mars 5,* an orbiter, is successful.

Skylab is launched.

Mariner 10 completes flybys of Venus and Mercury.

1974 — The USSR continues lunar unpiloted exploration with the *Luna 22* lunar orbiter, which is successful, and *Luna 23,* which fails.

1975 — The USSR launches *Venera 9* and *Venera 10,* Venus orbiter/landers.

NASA launches *Viking 1* and *Viking 2,* Mars orbiter/landers.

1976 — The USSR collects lunar samples with *Luna 24.*

1977 — The first Space Shuttle orbiter, *Enterprise,* flies in tests atop a 747 and later in free-flight tests. *Voyager 2* sets out for flybys of Jupiter, Saturn, Uranus, and Neptune.

Voyager 1 sets out for flybys of Jupiter and Saturn.

1978 — *Pioneer Venus 1* sets out to orbit Venus.

Seasat A begins global observations of the Earth's oceans.

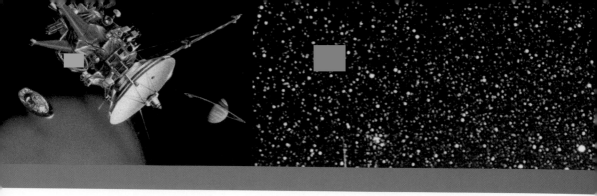

Pioneer Venus 2 sends probes to the surface of Venus.

The USSR's Venus explorations continue with orbiter/landers *Venera 11* and *Venera 12*.

1981 — NASA launches the first Space Shuttle flight. Columbia is piloted by astronauts John W. Young and Robert L. Crippen. It is the first airplanelike spacecraft to land on Earth from orbit.

1986 — An explosion destroys the Space Shuttle *Challenger.* All seven members of the crew die. A long investigation and redesign process follows.

1988 — The Space Shuttle returns to flight with the twenty-sixth shuttle flight, made by the spacecraft *Discovery.*

1989 — The *Magellan* Venus orbiter is launched. This highly successful mapping mission lasts 4 years.

NASA launches the orbiter/probe *Galileo* to study Jupiter.

1990 — The Hubble Space Telescope is launched from the Space Shuttle.

Ulysses sets off on its mission to fly by Jupiter and head toward the Sun. Eventually, it will orbit the Sun's poles.

1992 — NASA launches, but then loses contact with, *Mars Observer*.

1994 — The *Clementine* spacecraft is launched to orbit the Moon and complete an asteroid flyby.

1996 — The *NEAR* (Near Earth Asteroid Rendezvous) sets off to study the asteroid Eros.

Mars Global Surveyor, an orbiter, and *Mars Pathfinder*, with a lander and rover, are sent to Mars.

1997 — NASA launches the *Cassini* Saturn orbiter and *Huygens* Titan probe.

1998 — NASA launches *Lunar Prospector* to orbit the Moon.

Deep Space 1 sets off to fly by an asteroid and a comet.

Mars Surveyor '98 Orbiter (Mars Climate Orbiter) is launched. It does not accomplish its mission.

1999	*Mars Surveyor '98 Lander (Mars Polar Lander)* and *Deep Space 2* Mars penetrator are launched. Both are lost.
	NASA launches *Stardust,* which will collect a sample of a comet and return to Earth.
2003	Space Shuttle *Columbia* breaks apart while returning from its mission.

ballistic missile—a type of guided missile. During the first part of its flight, the missile's rocket engine propels it to a planned flight path. When the ballistic missile is on course, its engine shuts off. The missile coasts through the second part of its flight and then free-falls until it hits the atmosphere and burns up.

biosphere—the entire Earth, including all the organisms that live here, and everything that makes life here possible

booster—a rocket used to give another rocket the acceleration it needs for takeoff. As their fuel is used up, booster rockets are discarded and fall back to Earth. Some empty booster rockets can be collected and reused.

corona—the hot, thin outer atmosphere of the Sun

cosmonaut—the Soviet equivalent of an astronaut

docking adapter—a device that makes it possible for two spacecraft to join together in space

extravehicular activity (EVA)—activity outside a spacecraft; space-walking

gravity assist—a maneuver in which a spacecraft circles a body in space and takes advantage of the object's gravitational pull to increase its acceleration

greenhouse gas—a gas in a planet's atmosphere that allows the Sun's light to enter, but does not let heat escape

liquid fuel—a fuel, such as liquid oxygen, that exists naturally in a liquid state. A liquid-fuel rocket is very powerful and can be stopped and restarted, but is more complicated and expensive to build than a solid-fuel rocket. The Space Shuttle's main engines are liquid-fuel rocket motors.

liftoff—the ascent of a spacecraft from a launchpad

meteoroid—a rocky or metallic object of relatively small size, usually once part of a comet or asteroid. When a meteoroid enters Earth's atmosphere, it appears as a glowing streak in the sky and called a meteor.

multistage rocket—a rocket package that makes use of one or more booster rockets to provide additional lift

nova—a star that suddenly increases its light output and then fades away *orbit*—the path followed by an object as it revolves around another body

oxidizer—a material that supplies oxygen so that combustion can take place in a rocket engine

recoil—the kickback of a gun when it is fired

rendezvous—(verb) to meet, to be in the same area at the same time; (noun) a meeting or encounter

rocket thruster—a rocket used to change directions

satellite—any object that orbits another object in space. The Moon is a satellite of Earth, and Earth is a satellite of the Sun. Human-made satellites are called "artificial" to distinguish them from natural satellites, such as moons.

solar wind—a plasma, or ionized gas, that originates in the Sun's corona and is found throughout the solar system

solid fuel—a fuel that is a powder or solid material and contains its own supply of oxygen. Gun powder is one example. Solid-fuel rockets are much simpler and cheaper to make than liquid-fuel rockets, but they cannot be turned off or controlled once they've been started. The Space Shuttle's giant strap-on boosters are solid-fuel rockets.

suborbital—describes a rocket that does not travel fast enough to escape from Earth's gravity. It falls back to Earth rather than beginning to orbit around Earth.

vacuum—a space or volume that contains nothing at all, not even air

The news from space changes fast, so it's always a good idea to check the copyright date on books, CD-ROMs, and video tapes to make sure that you are getting up-to-date information. One good place to look for current information from NASA is U.S. government depository libraries. There are several in each state.

Books

Campbell, Ann Jeanette. *The New York Public Library's Amazing Space: A Book of Answers for Kids.* New York: John Wiley & Sons, 1997.

Cole, Michael D. Challenger: *America's Space Tragedy.* (Countdown to Space) Springfield, N.J.: Enslow Publishers, Inc., 1995.

_____. *Apollo 11: First Moon Landing.* (Countdown to Space) Springfield, N.J.: Enslow Publishers, Inc., 1995.

_____. *Apollo 13: Space Emergency.* (Countdown to Space) Springfield, N.J.: Enslow Publishers, Inc., 1995.

Launius, Roger D., and Bertram Ulrich. *NASA and the Exploration of Space: With Works from the NASA Art Collection.* Foreword by John Glenn. New York: Stewart, Tabori, and Chang, 1998.

Miller, Ron. *The History of Rockets.* Danbury, CT: Franklin Watts, 1999.

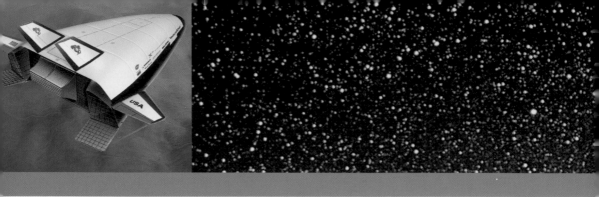

Mullane, R. Mike. *Do Your Ears Pop in Space?: And 500 Other Surprising Questions About Space Travel.* New York: John Wiley & Sons, 1997.

_____. *Liftoff! An Astronaut's Dream.* Parsippany, N.J.: Silver Burdett, 1994.

Neal, Valerie, Cathleen S. Lewis, and Frank H. Winter. *Spaceflight: A Smithsonian Guide.* (Smithsonian Guides Series). New York: Macmillan, 1995.

Ride, Sally, and Susan Okie. *To Space and Back.* New York: Lothrop, Lee and Shepard, 1989.

Scott, Elaine. Adventure in Space: *The Flight to Fix the Hubble.* Illustrations by Margaret Miller. New York: Hyperion Press, 1995.

Spangenburg, Ray, and Diane Moser. *Exploring the Reaches of the Solar System.* (Space Exploration) New York: Facts On File, Inc., 1990.

_____. *Living and Working in Space.* (Space Exploration) New York: Facts On File, Inc., 1989.

_____. *Opening the Space Frontier.* (Space Exploration) New York: Facts On File, Inc., 1989.

_____. *Space People from A to Z.* (Space Exploration) New York: Facts On File, Inc., 1990.

Spangenburg, Ray, and Diane K. Moser. *Wernher von Braun: Space Visionary and Rocket Engineer.* (Makers of Modern Science Series) New York: Facts On File, Inc., 1995.

Organizations and Online Sites

Many of the online sites listed below are NASA sites, with links to many other interesting sources of information about moons and planetary systems. You can also sign up to receive NASA news on many subjects via e-mail.

Astronomical Society of the Pacific
http://www.astrosociety.org
390 Ashton Avenue
San Francisco, CA 94112

The Astronomy Café
http://itss.raytheon.com/cafe/cafe.html
This site answers questions and offers news and articles related to astronomy and space. It is maintained by NASA scientist Sten Odenwald.

NASA Ask a Space Scientist
http://image.gsfc.nasa.gov/poetry/ask/askmag.html#list
Take a look at the Interactive Page where NASA scientists answer your questions about astronomy, space, and space missions. This site also has access to archives and fact sheets.

NASA Newsroom
http://www.nasa.gov/news/newsroom/index.html
This site features NASA's latest press releases, status reports, and fact sheets. It includes a news archive with past reports and a search button for the NASA website. You can even sign up for e-mail versions of all NASA press releases.

National Space Society
http://www.nss.org/
600 Pennsylvania Avenue, S.E., Suite 201
Washington, DC 20003

Planetary Missions
http://nssdc.gsfc.nasa.gov/planetary/
At this site, you'll find NASA links to current and past missions. It's a one-stop shopping center to a wealth of information.

The Planetary Society
http://www.planetary.org/
65 North Catalina Avenue
Pasadena, CA 91106-2301

Sky Online

http://skyandtelescope.com

This is the website for *Sky and Telescope* magazine and other publications of Sky Publishing Corporation. You'll find a good weekly news section on general space and astronomy news. Of special interest are *Sky and Telescope* feature stories adapted especially for online reading. The site also has tips for amateur astronomers as well as a nice selection of links. A list of science museums, planetariums, and astronomy clubs organized by state can help you locate nearby places to visit.

Welcome to the Planets

http://www.jpl.nasa.gov/solar_system/planets/planets_index.html

This tour of the solar system has lots of pictures and information. The site was created and is maintained by California Institute of Technology for NASA/Jet Propulsion Laboratory.

Windows to the Universe

http://www.windows.ucar.edu/tour/link=/windows3.html

This NASA site, developed by the University of Michigan, includes sections on "Our Planet," "Our Solar System," "Space Missions," and "Kids' Space." Choose from presentation levels of beginner, intermediate, or advanced. To begin exploring, go to the URL and choose "Enter the Site."

Places to Visit

Check the Internet (*skyandtelescope.com* is a good place to start), your local visitor's center, or phone directory for planetariums and science museums near you. Here are a few suggestions.

Exploratorium
3601 Lyon Street
San Francisco, CA 94123
http://www.exploratorium.edu/
You'll find internationally acclaimed interactive science exhibits, including astronomy subjects.

Jet Propulsion Laboratory (JPL)
4800 Oak Grove Drive
Pasadena, CA 91109
http://www.jpl.nasa.gov/pso/pt.cfm
JPL is the primary mission center for all NASA planetary missions. Tours are available once or twice a week by arrangement.

NASA Goddard Space Flight Center
Code 130, Public Affairs Office
Greenbelt, MD 20771
http://pao.gsfc.nasa.gov/vc/index.html
Visitors can see a Moon rock brought back to Earth by Apollo astronauts as well as other related exhibits.

National Air and Space Museum
7th and Independence Ave., S.W.
Washington, DC 20560
http://www.nasm.edu/nasm
This museum, located on the National Mall west of the Capitol
building, has all kinds of interesting exhibits.

Space Center Houston
Space Center Houston Information
1601 NASA Road 1
Houston, Texas 77058
http://www.spacecenter.org/
Space Center Houston offers a tour and exhibits related to humans
in space, including the Apollo missions to the Moon.

Index

Bold numbers indicate illustrations.

Ray Spangenburg and **Kit Moser** are a husband-and-wife writing team specializing in science and technology. They have written 33 books and more than 100 articles, including a five-book series on the history of science and a four-book series on the history of space exploration. As journalists, they covered NASA and related science activities for many years. They have flown on NASA's Kuiper Airborne Observatory, covered stories at the Deep Space Network in the Mojave Desert, and experienced zero-gravity on experimental NASA flights out of NASA Ames Research Center. They live in Carmichael, California, with their two dogs, Mencken (a Sharpei mix) and F. Scott Fitz (a Boston Terrier).